PRAISE FOR
FLYING LEAD CHANGE

"As someone who has spent their career working to create unstoppable cultures, I am thrilled that Kelly has written a book like *Flying Lead Change*. With an approach that focuses on principles from the equine world—care, connection, and joy—she has created a culture guide for leaders. When put into practice, these principles have the potential to not only impact teams and organizations, but families and communities as well. This book is such a gift!"

GINGER HARDAGE
former Senior VP of Culture and
Communications for Southwest Airlines

"*Flying Lead Change* is unique and extraordinary. It integrates wisdom with the practical, inspiration with proven research, and laughter with tears. Contemporary leaders who heed the advice and guidance of ancient wisdom will gain essential advantages and be forever changed. It is the clear promise of this book."

MICKI MCMILLAN, MCC
CEO and founding partner of Blue Mesa Coaching

"After spending time with Kelly at the EQUUS ranch in Santa Fe, it comes as no surprise that she has written a book that's a true game changer for leaders. *Flying Lead Change* brings together the age-old wisdom of the natural world with the newest data on neuroscience. The result is a guide that is both inspiring and practical—a must-read for any leader who longs to create lasting change in their organization and discover lasting joy while doing so. Kelly's book will awaken your heart and mind to what it means to be truly human on the 'great wild ride of life.'"

JAYSON TEAGLE
CEO of Collideoscope

FLYING LEAD CHANGE

KELLY WENDORF

FLYING LEAD CHANGE

56 MILLION YEARS OF WISDOM FOR LEADING AND LIVING

sounds true
BOULDER, COLORADO

Sounds True
Boulder, CO 80306

Published 2020

Cover design by Jennifer Miles
Book design by Meredith March

Printed in Canada

Library of Congress Cataloging-in-Publication Data

Names: Wendorf, Kelly, author.
Title: Flying lead change : 56 million years of wisdom for leading and
    living / Kelly Wendorf.
Description: Boulder : Sounds True, Inc., 2020. | Includes bibliographical
    references.
Identifiers: LCCN 2020006362 (print) | LCCN 2020006363 (ebook) | ISBN
    9781683645726 (paperback) | ISBN 9781683645740 (ebook)
Subjects: LCSH: Leadership. | Self-actualization (Psychology)
Classification: LCC HD57.7 .W45456 2020 (print) | LCC HD57.7 (ebook) |
    DDC 658.4/092--dc23
LC record available at https://lccn.loc.gov/2020006362
LC ebook record available at https://lccn.loc.gov/2020006363

10 9 8 7 6 5 4 3 2 1

For
my beloved Scott,
my exceptional son Dakota,
my powerful daughter MacKenzie,
and my magical mother Peta.

And for Cimarron, our teacher and friend.

CONTENTS

A LETTER
FROM THE AUTHOR

Out on the street. This was our prospect in the winter of 2018 when our landlord, a multibillion-dollar-backed investment firm, threatened to take away our ranch just outside of Santa Fe, New Mexico, due to a loophole in the contract. This was not only our family home, including a menagerie of animals, but also the retreat campus of our leadership and personal development organization EQUUS. Like so many business owners, Scott and I had poured everything we had into EQUUS—mind, body, soul. To lose our land now would be a disaster. Was this the end of it all?

After yet another cold, sweat-drenched night, I sat down to my desk in my study—a room reserved solely for my writing (and the occasional house guest). I sat blankly in front of my screen, my heart draining out of my feet. No words were flowing. Just then the phone rang. A kind voice spoke on the other end.

"Hi, my name is Anastasia."

"Yes . . ." I said flatly.

"I'm from Sounds True publishing. We wondered if you would be interested in writing a book for us."

And so began these pages. Life has been like that for me. I usually have to be tapped firmly on the shoulder by someone who sees the value in what I do and asked to step forward and share, sometimes despite my own pervading self-doubt. You could say I have a quality of reluctance.

The truth is, I used to be reluctant about simply being human. As a child, the disconnection, frustration, fear, betrayal, confusion, heartbreak, complexity, and challenges that invariably came along with being human overwhelmed me. Ambivalent about the entire experience, I was not altogether sure if I even wanted to be one—a human,

I mean. It seemed so much easier to be, say, an eagle or a deer, a tree, or nothing at all. I regularly questioned the status quo of what we were meant to value and strive toward. And though as a young adult working in the corporate sector I looked successful, internally I was besieged with conflict. This kindled a voracious drive to seek insight and answers so that I could thrive at being human and live by a code that felt intrinsically congruent. This book is a culmination of that lifelong education.

My seeking took me to some very unconventional places, and my path moved like a spiral, never direct, always winding from the inside out and from the outside in. It called forth teachers that emerged from several different and unlikely sources, teachers who have taken a variety of shapes and forms. The natural world has taught me more about being human than any person could, and the precious company of indigenous elders around the world taught me how to translate those invisible teachings of nature into practical applications of daily life. I spent years in India, immersed in the practice of spiritual self-inquiry with a sage in Uttar Pradesh. As the founding editor of an Australian magazine called *Kindred* (which explores the evidence-based conditions that create a just and sustainable society), I immersed myself in studying the field of neuroscience and learned about the biology of thriving. *Kindred* provided me the opportunity to explore the scientific underpinnings of all I had learned from nature, my spiritual work, and the indigenous teachings. And finally, the formal training in becoming a Master Certified Coach taught me to hold space for others on this human journey so that they too could find their way to live, guide their families, and lead their organizations from their own intrinsic wisdom. EQUUS is the full expression of that spiral-shaped journey; we use all those elements in our work with our clients and strive to embed them in our organizational culture.

You may not be as reluctant as I have been, but I'm fairly certain if you are human then you have had—and will have—your fair share of challenges that we all invariably face. Perhaps, like me, you are looking for trustworthy answers and insights and, like me, you have had your fill of conventional approaches to problem-solving and want something that resonates more harmoniously with some quiet calling within you.

This book is a field guide to being human. It weaves together the influences of nature-based intelligence, indigenous knowledge, contemplative wisdom, and neuroscience for a new reality. In it you will meet a number of teachers, and you will have the opportunity to learn from them too, just as I did (and still do). Additionally, you will receive applications and practices so that the teachings translate into lasting change and transformation in your own life, with your family, and for your work. I hope that you will recognize the book's invitation as not only an individualized growth opportunity, but a chance to influence a larger constituency, for we are shaped not only by our private choices, but our lives are coauthored by the cultural milieu within which we abide.

For those of you who are looking for a quick how-to guide, who prefer succinct bullet lists and mental model diagrams, this is a heads up. The type of wisdom that sustains over time and translates into practical measurable change does not deliver first to the mind. It delivers to the heart. According to neurocardiologists, the heart and its complex neural network send more information to the mind than the mind sends to the heart.[1] When the heart informs the mind, the mind gains wisdom. The heart learns through story, through time, and through reflection. For this reason, this book deliberately traverses in such a way for you to learn *differently* for more optimal outcomes. Be prepared to settle in and travel the places it takes you; it may at times feel oddly not rational or linear.

To support your personal growth process, at the end of each chapter is a breakout section titled Spiral Point that features journal questions, suggested exercises, and reflections so that you too can journey from the inside out and the outside in. While I am not a neuroscientist, I do study the field because it's an effective pathway to learning and changing our brains, hence many of the exercises are based in the neuroscientific principles and include somatic (bodily, visceral, felt sense) instructions. Such somatic exercises help you to rewire your nervous system and your brain and therefore create lasting change in your life. When engaging with the exercises, I advise you to make small micro-steps toward change. Studies show that small, practical, easily practiced action steps create significant change over time, rather than huge efforts that invariably fall to the wayside.[2]

To protect the privacy of EQUUS clients and other individuals referred to in this book, some names have been changed and details excluded. The book includes traditional stories that have been passed down over time and therefore often can't readily be attributed or cited to an individual source, but I do my best to acknowledge my sources wherever possible. I have been sensitive to include only stories that have been freely shared, and have made sure to omit certain teachings not meant for public consumption. I also want to alert First Nations readers (specifically Aboriginal and Torres Strait Islander people) that this book contains images and names of people who have died.

And what happened to our property and EQUUS? Writing the book that became *Flying Lead Change* carried us through a personal and organizational turning point—another essential twist in the spiral. We emerged with our land, our family, our company, and our campus not only intact but prospering, and in the process experienced another profound validation of the principles outlined in these pages.

Wi don gi mu

(From the traditional Tewa language, meaning "We are one in mind, heart, and in the spirit of love for all.")

KELLY WENDORF, MCC, MECD
Santa Fe, New Mexico
January 2020

A broken song beneath the snow, the echo of a soaring joy, a shape in the mist, a touch in the rain, in wilderness you come again . . . you tell us what we used to know . . . you speak for all the free wild things whose ways were ours when the wind had wings.

ELISE MACLAY,
"When the Wind Had Wings"[1]

What Is a Flying Lead Change?

On a hot, humid afternoon, a small doglike creature nibbles on fruit suspended above a lush, fern-covered ground. The thick jungle forest is bursting with sound, as this is a time when mammal life explodes with innovative evolutionary options. Nearby our earliest ancestor (also small) moves past, vying for the same sweet delicacy. For a moment the two lock eyes.

Fifty-six million years later, in the same place we now call Wyoming, their descendants are working together in perfect harmony, human and horse, to move a herd of cattle off a northern slope into a grassy valley. As the horse gallops up a ridgeline, suddenly the topography changes, and the herd of cattle makes an abrupt directional shift. In response, the horse effortlessly executes what is known as a *flying lead change*—a gravity-defying maneuver that allows them to change balance and respond to the changing scenario without losing momentum or unseating their rider. Like this, horses have been our partner in successfully navigating change for thousands of years—the perfect power couple.

A flying lead change is the equestrian term for a high-level yet natural gymnastic move that happens at the canter, lope, or gallop (a horse's fastest gait). In lay terms, when a horse canters, they lead with either their left or right set of legs. Say you were watching this cowboy gallop up the ridge. You might see their horse reach with their left front leg farther than their right; that would indicate a left lead. Horses will remain in a particular lead (or at least favor one) and continue their trajectory in that manner. It is only by external influences—a radical change in topography, for example—that the horse will change leads.

The flying lead change, or *flying change* as it is sometimes called, is when the animal, midflight, changes their lead from left to right, or vice-versa. At its finest, when you are astride a highly trained horse who deliberately executes the motion with balanced elegance, a flying change is astonishing to experience.

A masterful feat of gravity defiance that would be the envy of any prima ballerina or black belt, the flying change requires a culmination of complex and coordinated elements executed in one dynamic flow mid-air: attunement to change, connection, balance and equilibrium; a quiet mind; openness to new possibilities; tempo; a suspension of pattern while continuing momentum; and finally levitation to create space for a transition of balance and new direction.

> OUR TOPOGRAPHY IS RADICALLY CHANGING, WHICH REQUIRES US TO CHANGE THE WAY WE LEAD OUR LIVES, FAMILIES, AND ORGANIZATIONS.

Collectively we are facing the need for the same physics-defying maneuver. Our topography is radically changing, which requires us to change the way we lead our lives, families, and organizations. Such topography calls us to execute this change with similar mastery: attunement, care, presence, connection, mindfulness, openness to possibility, levity, suspension of old habits, maintaining momentum, levitation for a transition of balance into something new . . . humanity's flying lead change.

We need more than policy change; we need a collective change of heart, a turn of equilibrium, a radical shift in the dynamics of how we do things. Together in this book we will explore the conditions, principles, and practicalities that will, in the midst of our ever-speeding lives, support us to change our lead midflight into a new way forward that will sustain us across the millennia as the horse has sustained itself for tens of millions of years.

This book is not about horses. It's about you and me listening together for a way of living and leading that is both practical and wise, as taught by an ancient successful system.

Introduction

Our Boeing 720 landed at the Addis Ababa International Airport. It was 1972 and Ethiopia, though on the verge of civil war, beckoned to those in search of the earliest record of humankind—scientists, academics, and explorers. My father was all three. Impatiently he waved at us from across the chain-link arrivals gate on the tarmac. His khaki-clad figure looked odd among the throngs of tall, dark, colorfully decorated bodies. My mother waved anxiously back and closely navigated my little brother and me down the airstairs, our small arms squeezed tightly in each hand.

A celebrated archaeologist, yet a complicated, tormented loner with narcissistic tendencies, my father was accustomed to spending most of his time in the preferred company of three-million-year-old stone tools, artifacts, and bones. One year, he decided we should spend some time with him in his world—the excavations on the side of a collapsed volcano known as Gademotta, in central Ethiopia.

Without much fanfare, he briskly ushered us through the large open concrete hall that was the airport. All around us was chaos and noise. Our rectangular Samsonite bags stood incongruously amongst burlap sacks, chickens and goats in wooden cages, and overstuffed baskets bound by rope and string. The hot air smelled of leather, smoke, sweat, and earth—a smell I recognized from the brightly beaded jewelry my father used to bring home from his travels.

All eyes stared at the two small, very blond white children amongst them—an extremely rare sight in that region of Africa in the early 1970s. People gathered around us, laughed, and exclaimed loudly as they touched our hair, felt the skin of our arms, and cradled our faces with their hands without thought of personal boundary.

I was an unusually observant seven-year-old. Too thin-skinned, my father would say, to societal norms. I was sensitive to the jagged undercurrent between my mother and father. I was distraught by a felled tree, a homeless animal, or a racist remark. When *Time* magazine featured that terrifying image of nine-year-old Kim Phuc running for her life from a napalm attack, my mother had to console me for countless nights. Serious and melancholic, I took on the gravity of my troubled family and a troubled world—perhaps in response to my father's self-absorption.

My only refuge was on the back of a horse. At age five I was placed atop my first—a magnificent chestnut thoroughbred named Pilgrim. Jane, my godmother and a seasoned horsewoman, walked him to our front yard on Saturday morning. Still in my pajamas, I bolted out the front door only to be scolded. "No running!" Jane commanded sternly as she hoisted me to settle into the soft, warm sway of Pilgrim's back. From that moment on I was inexorably consumed by anything to do with horses. In another culture, I might have been considered possessed by horse spirits.

My drawings of horses plastered my bedroom walls. A herd of plastic Breyer model horses of all shapes, colors, and breeds galloped across my bookshelves. My best friend Kayanne and I would prance around the front yards, tossing our manes—I the black stallion, she the fierce and sleek Arabian. My mother succumbed to years of driving me to riding lessons and finally purchased my first horse.

Our environment shapes us. Throughout my childhood, mine was a juxtaposition of two ancient worlds—that of my father's (the numerous archaeological digs and dwelling sites of various early indigenous peoples around the world) and that of my equine companions (their fields, forests, and mountains). Between those two settings I was intimately informed about life. Parented in the seventies in the Southwest by what I refer to warmly (and gratefully) as benign neglect—the style in those days—I was free to roam the outdoors on foot or on horseback until sundown. This meant I was either hunting for pottery shards and arrowheads inside a collapsed kiva (an ancient underground ceremonial chamber) or trotting bareback and barefooted down a stretch of dirt road. It was my secret domain, this ancient, earthen, animal way of being that I thought was uniquely my own. Until we went to Ethiopia.

We were driven into the heart of the drought-stricken country, although Ethiopia had not yet seen the full human tragedy destined to come with her looming famine. Children raced after our military jeeps as we passed villages—mud and straw huts surrounded by erect, colorfully beaded women. We drove on one of the few roads stretching between Addis Ababa and Nairobi to a small town called Ziway. The countryside was barren, ornamented with the occasional bent acacia tree—a scribble of green above a single crooked trunk amidst a sea of red clay.

Finally we arrived at a small, rectangular cinder-block building of about eight rooms, painted a bright blue and surrounded by an occasional tormented rosebush struggling through the hard, sunbaked earth. Named the Bekele Molla Hotel after its owner, it would be our home for the next few weeks. From there we would take our daily journeys with our father to the 235,000-year-old excavation sites in the Ethiopian Rift Valley.

To me, Ethiopia was beautiful. And the people were even more so. I remembered my cheeks hurting from smiling so much in their presence, how they made my heart tickle inside when they spoke to me in Cushitic, and how they made me laugh when they laughed at me good-naturedly. And that was even before I met Kabada.

Kabada walked with long, graceful strides behind my father, dwarfing my father's six-foot-four build. A white blanket slung elegantly over his right shoulder made him look like an emperor. A single dangling earring accentuated his jawline, his chin held high, his shoulders back. His wide feet met the earth with the snugness of belonging. In one hand was a spear, and in the other, a small metal lunch box.

My father hired Kabada, an Oromo warrior, to guard my brother and me at all times. Apparently two American children playing in the African bush were a kidnapping target in the local growing unrest. "It's for the baboons," Dad said, noticing me staring at Kabada's spear. He swept his arm along the landscape, indicating their probable whereabouts. "He will wedge the base into the sand, like this," he said, gesturing how the spear would be secured to the earth, angled toward the attacker, "and the sharp point will lodge into its chest when it pounces." My father completed the horrifying pantomime with a hand arching toward its death by finger-point. I of course was not so worried about myself as the poor unsuspecting baboon, simply wanting his dinner.

The Oromo are one of the indigenous peoples of East Africa and the largest ethnic group in Ethiopia. As is the fate of so many of the world's traditional peoples, the Oromo were (and continue to be) among the most persecuted during Ethiopia's political struggles, and they suffered severely during the two recent famines that claimed millions of lives, most of them Oromo. Today, thousands of Oromos are kept in secret concentration camps and jails just for being Oromo.[1]

Kabada watched over my brother and me with complete concern, as if we were the most important things on earth. He was gentle, with kind, quiet eyes. He stood by as we played in the dust of the excavation sites, propped against his spear—a silent sentinel—while archaeologists crouched busily nearby. At night as we slept, he stood alert outside our door under the porch light, moths flying around his head in zigzagging spirals.

In time, I convinced him that protection was only just part of his job description; the rest was to play with me. Obligingly he swung me around in circles and tossed me in the air. He drank tea alongside my teddy bear; he chased goats on my imaginary horse ranch. I grew warmly accustomed to Kabada, though not a single word was spoken between us, and I blended myself into the daily, colorful, laughter-infused clamor that was Oromo life.

One day my father took his team to a remote village and invited us along. The community was comprised of eight circular huts with thatched roofs, some white zebu cows, goats, and a number of smiling men, women, and children. The *sanacha* (elder or chieftain) of the village generously welcomed us. After exchanges of gifts and some conversation translated by my father's colleague, Bahai, the sanacha presented his treasured horse—a small grey decorated for the occasion with orange-red tassels and matching rope. In such communities, a horse is a symbol not only of noted leadership status, but of the owner's rarefied capacity to see between realms. It is believed among traditional peoples around the world that horses are messengers from the gods, and therefore they should be handled only by those worthy of such a sacred relationship.[2]

I desperately wanted to sit on that little horse. Perhaps even ride him around the village, or trot out across the bush and chase baboons. But my parents forbade it, telling me that as I was neither shaman, nor mystic, nor chieftain. For me to ask to do so would be highly disrespectful.

The sanacha then mentioned a village boy who had recently contracted an illness for which he was not recovering. Upon a brief examination by Dad's team members, it was clear the boy needed urgent medical attention. There was a brief discussion between everyone. At once the team moved to get the boy into a jeep and make the long journey on faded dirt roads to the nearest hospital, some hours away.

Days later we returned to the village with the healthy boy. The sanacha, overwhelmed, shook my father's hand vigorously. There was much commotion and singing. Suddenly two men whisked me up and astride the chieftain's horse. With that he put his hands on my father's shoulders and blessed our family, saying that we—and all those we loved and cared for—would be in the protection of his ancestral spirits forever. Though I was too young to understand the significance of that exchange, the blessing ripened in me over time and infused in me a sense of protection and social responsibility.

Me as a child on the chieftain's horse

Weeks later, we were set to depart our tiny motel home. The sun had not yet risen, and Kabada was still at his place by my door, moths flying around the exposed bulb hanging above his head. Only now he was sitting in a rusted metal chair, slumped over listlessly. Around him was much activity as the team loaded up their gear to go. Kabada sat stone still.

Not able to comprehend the situation, I jumped happily up on to his lap and squeezed him around the neck. I thought he would laugh in his usual way, but instead he pulled me in and held me tightly, his long arms wrapping completely around my small frame, his chest rising and falling falteringly against mine. He held me at length without a sound.

I pulled away slightly to look at his face. Tears ran down his cheeks, tiny rivulets streaming through the dust. It was the first time I had seen a man cry. Then I realized I might never see Kabada again. I curled back into the safe harbor of his embrace and began to melt into the tender exchange between us that was happening without words—a conversation between the ancient world and the new about care and responsibility. In that moment, we met across a chasm of time,

DO YOU REMEMBER A GENTLER TIME IN THE WORLD WHEN EVERY PERSON WAS SUPPORTED WITH SUCH AN INTRINSIC WHOLENESS?

language, race, and familial ties and without the slightest trace of separation or thought, merged into a state of unconditional love.

At some point in a person's life, if we are lucky, we might have such an uncommon opportunity, when the curtains of mental constructs part and we behold something precious, sacred, and true. Sometimes it can happen at the bedside of a dying loved one or while listening to a piece of music or in nature. Other, truer dimensions briefly penetrate through and leave us forever changed. Those weeks amongst the Oromo and that early morning experience with Kabada under the porch light forever changed me. They created an indelible internal compass setting toward unconditional love that would both inform and haunt me. It embedded an unmistakable calling, which I was compelled to follow for the rest of my life.

My guess is that you feel called, too, to something. And I'd bet that somewhere in your life some event set your inner compass to that calling, whether you were aware of it or not. This book is for the called. It is for thought leaders, visionaries, professionals, parents, creatives, and all those who care. It is for you who have seen or sensed another way and those of you who feel you are being asked to participate in humanity's flying lead change through the way you live and lead. For these are times that require not just social change in the traditional sense, but something magnificent—a civilizational sleight of hand, an artful change of foot midstride in a miraculous act of physics-defying thrust into the unknown.

What was revealed to me in Ethiopia can be best described by one word: connection—connection to oneself, to another, to existence. Do you remember a gentler time in the world when every person was supported with such an intrinsic wholeness? Neither do I. And yet we yearn for it as if we were exiles from a beloved homeland.

Over the span of my life, this yearning formed seminal questions for me personally and professionally: What does it mean to be human? What is the source of disconnection—and, conversely—connection? What are the consequences of a disconnected society—in life and in work? How do we create conditions to restore connection and wholeness? How do we elicit change inside behemoth forces that seem too large to repair? Looking for answers, I researched and searched. I traveled to and lived in vastly different societies and eventually immigrated to Australia. Through my travels and living abroad, I learned that culture plays an integral role in shaping our ideas about who we are as human beings. The modern post-industrialized culture's story, for example, is one of disconnection and separation. Its narrative creates a prison that affects our health, our thinking, our success, and now our very survival.

Eventually this exploration culminated in my founding *Kindred* magazine in Australia. *Kindred* sought to answer some of my questions. My work there exposed me to the latest social theories and brain science. It was there I learned about the brain's right and left hemispheres. While old science mistakenly attributed reason to the left hemisphere and emotion to the right, new science divides the two in a more nuanced fashion. Put simply, the left brain is about mechanics, rational thought, knowing, subject-object relationships, technology, and things. The right brain encompasses wholeness, connection, listening, the unknown, livingness, and embodiment. They offer two essential versions of the world. Neither side is perfect or better. True intelligence reigns when both sides of the brain work in concert with one another.

However, over the last century our culture has become increasingly left-brained. This is due to the fact that the left system can reinforce itself through all it knows. Because the left brain controls things like technology and the media, it's quite vocal on its own behalf. The right brain, dedicated to listening and the unknown, remains intrinsically silent in comparison. You could say all the ominous challenges of our time are a reflection of that imbalance. The left brain then tries to solve these problems through itself, throwing us into a deadly perpetual feedback loop.[3] We have lost our way.

I am not advocating for one side over the other. Both are essential. I'm arguing for a more balanced relationship in service of something beyond what the left brain could comprehend on its own. Optimally, the right brain inspires the left, and the left serves the whole by making manifest the right brain's intuitive wisdom in the world. Instead, the rational mind has become a tyrant master rather than a faithful servant.

While *Kindred* did much to enlighten its readers about the science-based approaches to connection, what was missing was specific right-brained and experiential wisdom available from the two most trustworthy resources that had accompanied me since childhood—horses and the wisdom of traditional peoples.

In response, my work took an abrupt right turn, so to speak. I cofounded EQUUS, a personal and professional development organization that seeks to connect people back to themselves through nature-based wisdom, and from that encounter transform their lives and their organizations. Owned and operated jointly with my partner J. Scott Strachan, our approach synthesizes equine integrated learning with other experiential processes informed by neuroscience, contemplative wisdom, and indigenous principles in order to ignite right-brained discovery. Our Experiential Discovery and Learning Campus—Thunderbird Ridge—sits at the foothills of the Sangre de Cristo mountain range. It is home to a herd of flamboyant horses (and a donkey) whose job is to facilitate clients toward their own awakening and, well, their own flying lead change. A flying lead change allows clients not only to switch leads to the right and access that right-brained genius, but to switch skillfully from one side to the other, depending on the topography. It thus allows them an expanded repertoire of solutions to solve their problems and create amazing lives of meaning and purpose that they never imagined possible.

And what's so special about working with horses? As you will learn in the pages of this book, horses elegantly organize themselves around seven principles: *care, presence, safety, connection, peace, freedom, and joy.* These principles assured their survival for millions of years, making them among the oldest and therefore most successful mammals on earth (only the echidna and platypus have them beat at about 100 million years).[4] Horses are highly relational to humans (unlike the platypus and echidna), making them consummate teachers of their ageless wisdom. When we are in their midst we become a part of the herd, and it therefore is incumbent upon them to teach us these fundamentals. It is these precepts that create the capacity to execute a flying lead change. The book is organized around these seven principles of this ancient system of thriving. Each part contains chapters outlining specific ways to implement these principles.

People come to EQUUS from diverse walks of life. But predominantly we serve those on the front lines of corporate America—the seemingly privileged few. Curiously, many come when they are out of options. They've sailed to the far edges of the societal seas, done everything by the book, earned success, power, and status. But to their dismay, they discover there is nothing there—no promised land, no happiness or meaning. The proverbial canaries in the civilizational coal mine, these people expose the toxicity of living according to the rules of a disconnected society. We would be wise to see the symptoms upon us now and quickly change our footing to another way forward.

This book gives voice to the right-sided realm. The quiet, open, connected, embodied, and the unknown. I don't advocate that indigenous and nature-based wisdom is better or perfect; I advocate that it allows us access to something we've lost.

One of my most influential teachers and close friends, whose wisdom informs the pedagogy of EQUUS, was an Australian Aboriginal named, respectfully, Uncle Bob Randall. A *tjilpi* (elder) from the Yankunytjatjara and Pitjantjatjara nations in the heart of Australia, he is one of the listed traditional keepers of Uluru, the enormous red rock known to most as Ayers Rock. As an Aboriginal man, Uncle Bob is a member of what is the oldest civilization in the world.[5] He was also a member of the Stolen Generations—the thousands of Aboriginal children kidnapped by missionaries to be raised by the government.[6] The policy, perversely called the Aboriginal Protection Act, sought to totally eradicate the Aboriginal race. As the Chief Protector of Aborigines in Western Australia, A. O. Neville wrote in an article for *The West Australian* in 1930: "Eliminate the full-blood and permit the white admixture to half-castes and eventually the race will become white."[7]

I first encountered Uncle Bob in 2008, while in Paris of all places. I was travelling with my then-husband and two young children and was several months pregnant with my third child. I was living in Byron Bay, Australia, as the founding editor of *Kindred* when a publisher asked me to compile an anthology of stories about belonging after reading an editorial I had written on the topic (again, tapped on the shoulder). So at the time I was collecting various essays from writers all around the world, some of them from indigenous writers. My once resilient marriage was now fragile and I hoped that our new baby might strengthen our ties. But the trip only provided more stress and we argued—a lot. One afternoon, as I climbed up a flight of narrow, creaking stairs to our simple hotel with my husband and children in tow, I began to miscarry. By the time I made it to our room, I had lost her.

What does one do with a dead child in a hotel room in Paris? In our shock, everything became oddly strange and remotely practical. We found an empty pastry box from our breakfast, carefully swaddled her in a napkin, and placed her inside. Like zombies, we walked with the little box to the only place that felt right—Notre Dame. We lit candles and held each other. As we emerged from the great cathedral, again we were faced with the question of what to do with her next.

Our eyes sadly landed on the Seine River. Without saying a word, my son looked up at me, went back inside the cathedral, and came out with a handful of small candles. We carried the box to the river's edge. On its lid, we placed the candles and some small flowers we gathered from bushes. We lit the candles, then we released the box into the current. I watched the Seine carry my last child out toward the sea. A part of me went down river with her into the abyss.

That afternoon we huddled around a café table, trying to pull ourselves together, feeling way too far away from home. I dully looked up over my tea at a bulletin board hanging over the counter. To my surprise there was a small poster promoting a community screening of an Australian film called *Kanyini* featuring Uncle Bob. As I looked upon Uncle Bob's face, a sudden thought pierced through my traumatized haze—I needed him in the belonging book. I made a mental note to myself to find him when I returned to Australia.

Tragedy can bestow enormous gifts if you are open to them. Had I not lost the baby, I probably never would have met Uncle Bob. As a white woman, I had no previous contact with Aboriginal Australians. The racial divide remains acute in Australia, and most white Australians never cross paths with Indigenous people, who are largely and conveniently tucked out of sight by governmental policy. When I returned home, a series of synchronistic events related specifically to the miscarriage landed me Uncle Bob's phone number, briskly scrawled in pencil by a friend-of-a-friend-of-a-doctor-of-a-colleague on a wrinkled yellow Post-it.

I finally worked up the courage to call the number. After several rings, Uncle Bob answered. Without as much as a *hello* he said, "I've been waiting for you to call." I was confused. I stammered a self-introduction and started to explain why I had called, but he interrupted, "It's time for people to hear what I have to say. Most of my people are too broken to carry on the teachings." He continued, "I was just sitting here wondering, *Now who am I meant to tell?* and you called, and so it's you I need to tell. And you will tell the others." He then laughed, as if he knew he was delivering yet another tap on my reluctant shoulder.

I had the incredible fortune of having much time in Uncle Bob's company over several years until his passing in 2015. He would speak to me at length with stories or teachings. Yet often we would go hours, sometimes days, without words, which was another kind of instruction.

One morning while sitting over coffee in a busy urban cafe, Uncle Bob was telling me yet another story. The paradox suddenly struck me. Here I was amidst the whirl of modern life, listening to a story that had been handed down for tens of thousands of years, a story that spoke about connection to place, to spirit, and to family, as well as our responsibility to all living things as administered to us through unconditional love.

The people hurried past us—carrying their briefcases, talking loudly on their cell phones—a spin of stress, speed, and anxiousness. And yet what Uncle Bob was living, what he was trying to convey to me, was something utterly forgotten by our society.

I began to cry. Confused, Uncle Bob stopped speaking. "What's wrong?" he asked.

"Your people lost everything. *Everything* was taken from you."

"Are you crying for my people?" he asked. I shook my head. I was crying for mine.

"Uncle Bob, I don't want to be disrespectful. But your people, they know what they lost. And if they don't know, they know they lost *something*."

He nodded carefully.

"We don't even know that we've lost something. That's how lost we are."

Uncle Bob hadn't thought of it that way. And as the world frenzied around us, we wept quietly together, holding hands. Both of us grieving for the entire human race.

"When you get lost," Uncle Bob told me some months later while taking me to the very site he was stolen as a child, "you retrace your steps to the place where you were before the lost-ness started." Without words, he then drove me some hours deeper on a dusty red road into the outback. Finally we came to a cut in the fence line, drove into a small clearing, and parked. He got out of the vehicle and started walking through the bush. I followed. We came to a place where the land sloped down, and at the bottom was a *billabong* (a water hole). Uncle Bob then sat down behind some *munyunpa* bushes about a hundred yards from the water's edge.

"Why are we here?" I whispered, as I sat down too, not knowing why I was whispering. Uncle Bob said nothing.

Then a few moments later, I heard a thundering sound and saw billows of red dust in the distance. Over the rise galloped about thirty wild horses—mares and babies, stallions, young and old, bays, chestnuts, greys, and blacks. They gathered nervously at the water. Some started to drink. Some blew mighty snorts, their heads raised in alarm—they knew something was out there. We sat utterly still, hardly breathing.

I had never told Uncle Bob I was a horsewoman. And I never told him I was inexorably adrift inside the traumatic loss of a child—a grief so all-consuming I was drowning. Or that I was in the throes of yet another divorce that threatened to destroy not only my family, but my career. Or that I had turned my back on my entire spiritual life after suffering at the hands of an unscrupulous narcissistic spiritual teacher. I felt exiled from my entire life. Sitting in the swell of the billabong, at the end of the world, in the middle of nowhere, I knew I was at rock bottom.

"There," he finally said, gesturing to the herd, "that mob there will get you home again."

With Uncle Bob in 2008

I didn't realize it at the time, but that moment watching the wild horses began my return to myself, and with it the braiding together of all the key influences in my life: horses, contemplative wisdom, my interest in neuroscience, and indigenous knowledge. The braid of those influences fused into one integrated whole through which I reclaimed my heart.

I wrote *Flying Lead Change* to help take us back to where we were before the lost-ness started, before we were taken from our collective knowing of connection—our very humanity. From there, it puts us on the right footing for transformation, for that leap into a change of lead. *Flying Lead Change* contains the material from my countless hours in the company of Uncle Bob and other respected traditional elders, trusted spiritual teachers, and the over fifty years in the wise and profoundly rigorous company of our most loyal companion, *Equus caballus*—the horse. All of this wisdom is grounded throughout the book in the evidence-based principles of neuroscience.

I do not presume to be, nor do I attempt to be, an expert in indigenous wisdom. I've done my best to be a listener. I do believe, however, that my time in the uncompromising tutelage of horses has influenced me toward a way of listening and translating that is trustworthy. The conversations, stories, insights, and teachings that were offered to me firsthand through the generosity of both horse and human were never meant for me alone. These pages are simply a passing on of that which must be shared, for you who are called to take flight into a new paradigm of living and leading. I sense there is a reason I have been exposed to a unique set of circumstances, woven between the natural worlds of the horse and the indigenous peoples of the earth that offer us a return to our own true nature.

There are many stories in this book—stories handed down, stories about the victory of the human heart in the company of horses, and stories about courageous people making a difference. Storytelling—the handing down of story and teaching—is a potent, trustworthy, and eternal form of instruction. Deceptively simple, story is a powerful device that serves as common ground across cultures. Such sacred words have a life of their own and move like a river, cutting their own way, leading to where they want to go.

It is my hope that the content of this book feels both relevant and respectful. And that it offers restoration of connection, equipping us to take that flying change of lead to live our lives and our organizations with the entirety of our whole-brain intelligence—right and left, heart and mind. If you are pulled to read this book, the words enclosed were meant specifically for you and are handed respectfully from our most ancient brothers and sisters through these pages to you. May you find the balance, courage, and strength to fly, on behalf of humanity and the world.

PART I
Learning to Listen

So let this winter
of listening
be enough
for the new life
I must call my own.

DAVID WHYTE,
"The Winter of Listening"[1]

When you are called, you are asked to listen. Before we learn about a sacred, ancient system to guide us, we must first know how to truly hear—not to words and paragraphs, but to the silence inside moments. As if walking into the quiet of a snow-blanketed forest, we enter into a stillness of mind, a hibernation of ego, that allows the subtler voices of wisdom to speak to us while other, louder faculties lie dormant.

When we truly listen, we suspend what we think we know. We cease resorting to a world rationally constructed of our past experience and instead pause over the infinite possibility granted by not-knowing. Here is where true change begins. Here in the winter of listening lives innovation, creativity, transformation, and invention.

Listening is the precursor to executing a personal and societal flying lead change. We poise ourselves toward and attune to the environment around us and take in all the information without filtering it through our preferences or biases.

In the following two chapters I invite you to bend your ear to another way of navigating inside your life, your work, and your family. You will receive new information that perhaps you've never considered before to prepare you for the real instruction ahead through the wise system of *care, presence, safety, connection, peace, freedom,* and *joy.* To find that way, I suggest slowing down and opening yourself to new possibilities through ancient voices, human and animal.

Chapter 1

The Promise

Let's go back to the beginning, to the place we were before the lost-ness started. To do that, we can retrace our footsteps back in time, beyond our own personal memory, into the collective ancient memory of our ancestors. In this collective memory has been embedded a promise to us that we are held, seen, and assisted to thrive for generations to come. Here we come to rely on stories that have been passed down for tens of thousands of years.

Original peoples across the continents have counseled through stories. Robin Wall Kimmerer—botanist, professor of plant ecology, and member of the Citizen Potawatomi Nation—writes that her people's stories are not so much commandments or rules, but "rather they are like a compass: they provide an orientation but not a map."[1] Stories like these are listened to in a different way, not with the rational mind but the heart.

Perhaps the most poignant and paradoxically timely story for our purposes is the following tale I heard from three different members of the Northern Pueblos of New Mexico (the Puebloans, or Pueblo peoples, are Native Americans of the Southwest and are largely a farming culture). A version of the story was also told to me by my father who heard it from a member of the Apache. I will say that this story belongs not only to the indigenous people of the Southwest, but also to the horses themselves, who have whispered it to me in their way. The story is poignant and relevant, because it tells of a tender and enduring kinship between horse and humankind and details the critical precipice on which we find ourselves today. In some traditions the story is called "Star Horse" or "The Time of the Great Outwaiting" or "The Return of the Horse." It is a teaching story, and it offers guidance for finding a path through our challenges. Below is my version, pieced together through the various accounts I have heard. I call it "The Promise."

This story begins like countless others that have been passed down throughout the ages: *A long time ago . . .*

when people first walked this land, the people and the animals all lived together in harmony. All the creatures and all living things were friends to the people. The birds, the reptiles, and the four-legged creatures all were friends. Even the insects, rocks, rivers, and trees were friends to the people. All the creatures and all the people would regularly gather in a circle to counsel one another and to celebrate their life on earth.

There was one creature in particular who was the most beloved of the people. This creature was the horse. It was said that horses were born from the sun and the stars, that they were messengers between heaven and earth. They were given to the people as a gift from the Creator, as a promise that the horses would guide and help them. So the people not only loved the horses but revered them. No one tried to train or domesticate a horse. They were sacred partners. In fact, there was no word for *horse* then. The creature was given a sacred word. A word that cannot be spoken. Back in those days horses were much smaller, not like the horses of today. And the people were small too. You would often see the horses and the humans walking or running together, sharing food, and sharing stories.

The horses were wise companions, and the people respected their point of view. Each day the horses and the people would greet one another in that sacred way that all creatures greet one another—with their breath. Mouth to nostril, in intimate connection, one would blow to the other. This greeting with the breath said, "I greet that in you, which is the same in me." This breath, this life force, is the same in all living beings. It is a salutation of oneness and the recognition that we are all from the same livingness.

In those days, everyone lived in harmony together and everything worked well together. All things were in balance.

Over time, as the population of the people grew and they needed more resources, their farming and hunting practices fell out of balance. Concerned, the animals asked the horses to counsel their human friends. The horses agreed.

When the circle convened, the horses and the people greeted one another in their customary way—with an exchange of breath, mouth to nostril.

"Brothers, sisters . . . greetings to you, our beloved friends," said the horses.

"Greetings, dear friends," replied the people.

"It has come to our attention that your farming and hunting practices have grown out of harmony with the earth and all living things. You are hurting many. You are hurting us. And you are hurting yourselves," said the horses.

The people listened politely.

"If you continue, you will cause harm and a great darkness will descend upon us all," warned the horses.

But the people had grown arrogant in their thinking and they brushed off the warning and continued doing what they were doing, weaving a thread of fear and separation upon the land. As the horses predicted, a time of darkness indeed descended upon the earth. The land retaliated with drought and floods. Disease spread, and there was death and starvation. All the animals fled, including the horses.

No one quite knows where the horses went. Some say they moved further north. Some say they went back to the stars. Yet, one last horse remained. Before he departed to follow the others, he turned back to speak to one person—the only human who was still listening.

Breathing into her face, the horse spoke, "Greetings, dear sister. Our warning has come to be. This land is no longer safe for us, so we are leaving. But know this, dear friend. One day we will return, and when we do, it will begin a new time, a time of the *Great Outwaiting* where all of creation will sit at a crossroads between darkness and light. All of creation will be suspended and waiting to see which will prevail: dark or light. And humanity will decide. You humans will face a critical decision on behalf of us all—will you continue to live in fear and separation, or choose to live in love and connection?"

And with that, the last horse turned away and disappeared.

And so began a prophecy. It was told from grandmother to granddaughter to great granddaughter and from grandfather to grandson to great grandson. It was told in the kivas and council circles and whispered under blankets between children at night. It was told by the horses too, amongst themselves on vast plains and in forests. Everyone anticipated this time when all the creatures would wait to see which force would prevail: love and connection or fear and separation.

Thousands of years passed. Oceans rose; oceans receded. Ice spread; ice receded. And during this time, not a creature would speak to the humans, and the land was hostile, and there was much sadness.

Then one day, as the people gathered shellfish on the beach, they began to see large ships coming over the horizon. The ships anchored and smaller boats carrying large people clad in metal (and large creatures clad in metal, too) came to shore.

At first the people did not recognize the huge, metal creatures. There was so much fear in their eyes from the huge metal bits in their mouths and terrible spurs on their sides. These animals did not look like the small, peaceful animals from before. And the creatures also did not recognize the people at first, for the people were now much taller and had fear in their eyes, too.

But when the first horse stepped off the boat, he paused by one of the people on the beach and his breath fell upon the face of a young woman, which awakened an ancient memory in her.

"Oh, sweet brother, it is you!" she exclaimed. "It is you, our horse family, you have returned!" She and her clan fell to the ground in gratitude and respect because the prophecy had come to fruition. "You are back! Our beloved friends!"

It's interesting here to note that historically we are told that it was the might of the soldiers and their guns that inspired awe in the native people, but according to this story it was the reappearance of the horse that signaled the prophetic realization of a sacred story told for thousands of years that evoked so much veneration.

> The horses spoke to the people, and it began with the exchange of breath. "Greetings, dear brothers and sisters. We have returned. Thus begins the Time of the Great Outwaiting. What will you choose?"
>
> And the horses, because they were a promise from the heavens, because they were the most beloved of all the creatures, and because they were sacred and came from the sun and the stars, agreed to help the people live in love and connection and to choose wisely. But many people forgot the old ways, the old stories, and their ears and hearts were closed, and thus we are still in that time of waiting. All creation waits, looking upon humanity's final choice. And the horses are here, helping whomever will listen. They are the promise.

This story describes perfectly our relationship to horses throughout time. Indeed, they have partnered with us since the nascence of civilization, helping to till our soils, hunt, and travel across expanses. Yet new research into the history and prehistory of North America would have us reframe not only the history of the horse, but their wisdom and spiritual significance. Many traditions assert that, rather than being caught and domesticated, horses came to humans and offered themselves. North American indigenous cosmologies—including that of the Lakota, Diné (Navajo), Blackfoot, and Apache—assert that the horse is not merely livestock but a sacred wisdom companion given to humanity during a specific spiritual event, purposefully for our spiritual aid, to be venerated.[2] In contrast to the Eurocentric yet stubbornly perpetuated myth that horses were introduced to America by the Spanish, this story, like many indigenous horse-acquisition stories, aligns more with the real history of the horse.

In fact, the first horses on earth evolved on the North American grasslands 56 million years ago. The fossils of *dawn horses*, as they are called, show up ubiquitously across the continent. Paleontological page markers, their presence at a dig is like a chapter heading that indicates a remarkable time in earth's history, an epoch called the Eocene—when modern mammal families came into their own and spread worldwide. Dawn horses were small, often well under three feet high. At that time, we were small too.

Along with the earliest known horse fossil, paleontologists have found here in the same time period the earliest known fossil of a *euprimate*—a true primate. These fossils were discovered on a raised flat-topped area of land in Wyoming called Polecat Bench. This joint appearance of horses and primates together in the same locale and time frame is not coincidental, writes science journalist Wendy Williams in her account of the history of horses. As their prolific presence prancing across the art of the Ice Age reveals (horses are the most frequently represented animal in that period), long before we domesticated horses, we were close companions.[3] We are an evolutionary pair, a dynamic paleontological duo. "In those early Eocene days, we both enjoyed the same damp, hot, jungle-like environment, which isn't surprising given that we shared a common ancestor in the probably not-too-distant past," Williams writes.[4] There is plenty of evidence of this shared ancestor, but the easiest way to grasp the idea is to consider our common skeleton, though over time we each stretched in different directions for different reasons. "Today we look dissimilar," Williams continues, "but there was a time when we could have been mistaken for siblings."[5]

Horses and humans share tarsals and metatarsals, fibulas and tibias, and almost all the same bones, in what scientists call *biological kinship*. At some point, humans and horses evolved from the same stem animal. While it's not clear when this ancestral stem animal existed, some researchers point to over 100 million years ago. Thus, evolution—the great unfolding of life on our planet—is the foundation of the horse-human partnership, Williams writes, and the reason why we are capable of understanding each other so well. But for a very long while, that companionship was interrupted—at least for those prehistoric citizens in North America.[6]

About 8000 BCE, succumbing to climate change, disease, and increased human hunting, it is widely believed that horses departed from most parts of North America and migrated across the Bering Land Bridge into what is now Siberia.[7] For the people who remained, wherever they were, the times must have been dark indeed. The horses spent the next nearly ten thousand years galloping away, west across Asia into Europe and south to the Middle East and North Africa, to finally step off the ships of Spanish conquistadors.[8] Having traveled not only across space, but across an evolutionary arc of time, and shaped by global heat spikes, fluctuating ice ages, tectonic upheavals, volcanic mega-explosions, and other planetary forces, these horses were now much larger versions of their dawn ancestors.

The sense of time in ancient stories such as "The Promise" is much more elongated, and perhaps more accurate, than our modern sense. As I stand next to my mare Artemis, the view all the way back to our original meeting, in what is now Wyoming, millions of years ago is utterly disorienting.

As the story foretells, we are undeniably in a time of great waiting. We now collectively sit perched at the edge of our seats, watching what appears to be our last days. It's been a long yet anxious wait so far, one that began when conquerors landed on their final shore with weapons and war. Missiles poised, carbon levels rising, economies teetering. How is all this going to turn out? Will we survive? Will we transform?

We are offered help by a wisdom-companion who has masterfully learned the art of exceptional adaptation, flexibility, and survival. The wisdom they can offer us is one thing, our ability to receive it is quite another. This would require us to shift our view of horses as merely livestock, athletes, or pets and see them as they were intended—our sacred teachers. When a teacher emerges, listening is vital.

LOVE ABSENT LISTENING IS NOT LOVE.

In the fifty years I've worked alongside horses, I've trained across different disciplines—from reining to dressage, cross-country jumping to trail riding. Like most horse people, my approach to horses most of the time was one-sided. They were to conform to what

I requested. I had to be the boss. Eventually my skills evolved to including natural horsemanship. Loosely coined *horse whispering*, natural horsemanship created a more subtle connection with my horses and enlightened me to their acute sensitivity. But I remained restless in these approaches, dissatisfied with the hierarchy of human over horse. Even in horse whispering you're doing most of the talking; you're just not as loud. What was missing was the listening.

Then I purchased a horse named Dante from Cavalia, one of the largest traveling horse circus extravaganzas. Dante was a master at an invisible artform called *liberty work*. He frolicked around his human counterpart in an equine ballet of unfettered power. Mane and tail flying, he could pirouette, leap, run, rear, and circle around, all without carrot or stick. Dante awakened me from the trance of conventional horse practices. To understand Dante better, I began studying with some of the masters of liberty work (also called *liberty* for short).

Liberty is not a training method; it is a relationship. As the name suggests, the rapport is based in the freedom and sovereignty of the horse as a sentient being with their own desires and dignity. What transpires in true liberty work (there are counterfeits) is akin to exceptional musical improvisation through the engagement of raw unleashed equine power, resulting in an almost unbearable emotional exhilaration in both horse and human. Liberty has no horse and trainer, no subject or object. It is a dance of true connection. Liberty is the culmination of presence, patience, respect, and integrity. And it turned my world upside down.

There in the expanse of no round-pen, no reins, no ropes, no treats, no means of control or manipulation whatsoever, a horse could choose to connect and work with me, or not. In the beginning there was a lot of their choosing not to. I would leave the barn utterly defeated, climb into my car, and sob over my steering wheel. Humbled and sometimes literally on my knees in the arena, I threw away everything I had been taught about horsemanship. I became a willing student and listener of the horse. And so began the powerful instruction.

The trouble with our conventional relationship with horses across the ages is that it has been a one-way conversation, hinged on obedience. Regardless of how we say we love them, we aren't listening.

Not really. Love absent listening is not love. Strangely, in spite of our ages-old enchantment with horses, very little modern animal behavior theory has been applied to horses. Equine scientists have studied the best way to feed show horses, the best way to optimize the speed of race horses, the best way to solve lameness. But only recently has the natural behavior of horses been considered of true scientific interest. Exploiting their flight responses, we have driven and dragged horses into subjugation, into nothing less than slavery by spur, whip, and sugar cube. What is remarkable to me is how horses—in spite of their superiority in strength and size—compassionately oblige us and remain by our side. They made a promise, it would seem, to stick by us and help us, even if it meant bearing the consequences of our ignorance.

When I started listening to horses, something amazing happened. They started speaking. They started showing me a way of being that is powerful, but not *powerful over* (i.e., at the expense of others). They instructed me on the ways of the natural world and how to see the Invisibles: energy, thought, intention, and connection. Like a Zen master, they insisted on presence. And when I was off the mark, they didn't hesitate to show their strong disapproval.

WHAT IF YOU HAD A SOURCE OF WISDOM, A TEACHER, A MENTOR, WHO HAD BEEN AROUND FOR A REALLY LONG TIME AND WHO HAD MASTERED THE BIG CHALLENGES THAT WE ARE TRYING TO FIGURE OUT ABOUT HOW TO LIVE HERE ON EARTH?

I realized this instruction by the horses was available to anyone who was open—regardless of whether they liked horses or not—because the work is not about horses. It's about listening to an ancient wisdom teaching us to become a better human. So The EQUUS Experience® was created—an equine-integrated learning approach that partners people with horses to facilitate transformational change.

Horses ignore party lines, religious affiliations, race, gender, and class. Knowing only to reflect the truth, they mirror back to people who they truly are, minus the limiting stories and narratives that surround them. In the years of working with clients inside this process I have witnessed the miraculous as a result of this mirroring. Many people report they were mysteriously led to work with the horses and yet had no previous affinity to them. "It's almost as if I was recruited by them to be mentored," said one client, a senior leader of a health-care organization. This work is not about anthropomorphizing horses, but recognizing the wisdom they carry as sentient beings.

Robin Wall Kimmerer writes that in the Western tradition there is a recognized hierarchy of beings, with humans on top of course, and the plants and the rest of the animals at the bottom. It's becoming easier to imagine that this way of thinking is distorted, especially when we consider the presumed hierarchy white males have had over women and minorities. Human superiority over nature is just another conceit. "But in Native ways of knowing," Kimmerer continues, "human people are often referred to as 'the younger brothers of Creation.'"[9] It is understood that humans collectively have the least experience existing on earth and thus the most to learn.

"What if you had a source of wisdom, a teacher, a mentor, who had been around for a really long time and who had mastered the big challenges that we are trying to figure out about how to live here on earth?" asks my friend and founder of Biomimcry for Social Innovation, Toby Herzlich. "What would you ask?" Toby proposes that nature and the biological and ecological principles that are embedded in life itself could be that teacher. "I've always had the sense that there's a collective intelligence out there that we can learn from. Of all the species that have ever lived on earth, only one percent still remains; the other 99 percent have gone extinct or evolved into a new form. So that means that the organisms and systems that are around with us now are the survivors. They've honed ways of living together within the selection pressures and the challenges here on earth now. And they have a lot to teach us about how to be here for the long haul."[10]

It's time to listen to our elders. They come in the form of four legged, or winged, or rooted. Their voices are carried through the old traditional stories, around the world. As the story of "The Promise" suggests, our equine elders are actively enlisting us to learn from them so we can all thrive. They provide a compass setting to guide us toward a life that feels whole, dignified, and powerful.

While much research exists about the wisdom and health benefits of nature to humans, little is written about the reverse. But when we redefine our relationship to nature as recipients of its intelligence (rather than a master over its destiny), a reciprocity emerges that is constructive to all parties. In biology we call this a *mutualism*.

Journalist and professor at Harvard and UC Berkeley, Michael Pollan describes this elegant reciprocity. He writes that he stands inside a legacy of other gardeners, botanists, genetic engineers, and plant breeders who *breed*, *select*, and *develop*, rendering humans as the overlord and subject and plants as the object. But what if that grammar is all wrong? What if it's nothing more than a self-serving conceit? "A bumblebee would probably also regard himself as a subject in the garden and the bloom he's plundering for its drop of nectar as an object. But we know that this is just a failure of his imagination. The truth of the matter is that the flower has cleverly manipulated the bee into hauling its pollen from blossom to blossom."[11]

What would happen if we regarded our place in creation from the same upside-down perspective? In a coevolutionary relationship every subject is also an object, every object a subject. Then Pollan really stretches our minds, "That's why it makes just as much sense to think of agriculture as something the grasses did to people as a way to conquer the trees."[12]

Relevance is key to perpetuating the coevolutionary dance between species. To the degree that horses can remain relevant to us and us to them, we may benefit each other for countless more epochs. So this begs the question: Now that we no longer need them to toil in front of a plow, or gallop across a battlefield conquering yet another frontier do horses serve more than just pure selfish (and expensive) enjoyment for a small number of people? There in fact remains a frontier that we have yet to fully explore for which the horse is most qualified—the frontier of the human heart. And what are the horses shaping in us so that we all may survive? Am I training Dante when I move around him in the arena, asking for him to pick up a certain gait or circle around me? Or is he training me to be a better human—a human who is more open, more conscious, more present, and capable of ushering in a new world?

Though anecdotal, I've witnessed horses literally instruct and model for people how to live more consciously and powerfully. When horses are allowed to be in right relationship to us, absent conventional contexts, we then discover right relationship to ourselves. Here we can be teacher *and* student, giver *and* receiver, subject *and* object. Blur those lines and you find that binary thinking disappears into pure connection, right relationship to all things—ourselves, each other, and the entire universe.

Recognizing the connection that exists here and now with all things, we wade into the generosity—the commonwealth—of all life. I love this word *commonwealth*. It stresses interdependence and wealth as something to be allocated equitably, i.e., something to be shared in common.

Like the bee with the flower and like me with Dante, a *common wealth* is created—even without consciousness of it—through connection and reciprocity. These relationships with other humans or with natural communities connote notions of mutual respect and fairness, right relationship and well-being. The common wealth in this community of life on the earth now is clearly the evolutionary heritage and destiny that people share with other life forms.

To ensure our evolutionary destiny, let's ask for guidance from she who has expertly innovated and adapted for 3.8 billion years—Mother Nature. Can we have the humility to say to our plant and animal brothers and sisters, "We've lost our way, will you help us?" In the coming chapters, *Equus caballus* offers us many instructions, grounded in science and translated through the sensibilities of those who have known them the longest—First Peoples—on how to live our lives and lead our organizations in right relationship to the commonwealth of all life. Like the little dawn horse and their small two-legged companion, we can return to knowing that we all come from the same place, connected through time and space by invisible threads of shared legacy, spiraling together throughout eternity.

The story of "The Promise" implies a specific form of help at a specific time in our collective lives, given in a particular way. Can we, as a civilization, hear it?

SPIRAL POINT

JOURNAL QUESTIONS

- Are you called, or is something calling you now? If you were truly listening to that call, what is it?

- If you had a wise ancient mentor to assist you, what would you ask them?

EXERCISES

- Take yourself on a curiosity walk in nature. Wander amongst trees, a body of water, or a rock landscape and consider the possibility that the natural elements—clouds, water, trees, wind, or rocks—are animate beings that are relational to you and, as such, are instructive to you. What is that like? What do you discover?

- Practice deep listening, without categorizing the content as good or bad, significant or insignificant, etc. Listen intently to colleagues, friends, direct reports, and family members without jumping in, assuming, labeling, or being distracted. What do you learn?

Chapter 2

An Untamed Pedagogy for Life and Leadership

Though we are listening to ancient wisdom for guidance, it is not backward-looking or primitive, but a sophisticated system for contemporary times. As we reach bigger and faster through technological solutions to our problems, would it not be wise to also anchor ourselves to something that has mastered success on Earth for 56 million years? While this is not a system that is well-known or documented, it is one that slowly became evident to me through decades of listening to the instruction from the equine world.

It was Uncle Bob who taught me—not the system itself, but a way of being that would later allow me to finally see it clearly and be able to articulate it specifically as a template for living and leading. This happened in 2009 during one of my journeys to see Uncle Bob in his home village of Mutitjulu in the Northern Territory of Australia. The plan was for me to fly in, meet Uncle Bob, then together join a handful of other visitors and college students (about five of us total) for a camping trip "out bush."

Ayers Rock Airport serves those flying to the Australian center, where Uluru rises spectacularly out of the landscape. You can see it from the air when you fly in, and it is, as one would expect, breathtaking.

Uncle Bob met me at the front doors of the terminal, two bottles of water in his hand. I began to effuse the usual greetings. He just smiled. He handed me one of the bottles and walked to his four-wheel drive, an old white Land Rover turned nearly pink from years of driving on red clay. I followed behind and looked around for everyone else, curious why he wasn't speaking. He threw my bags in the back and got in the vehicle.

I jumped in and continued talking. Uncle Bob just smiled and nodded occasionally. Eventually my words couldn't withstand the emptiness they were tumbling into and just petered out. We drove in silence as he passed Mutitjulu and headed down a soft red-dusty dirt road, billows of red clouds in our wake. *Where was everyone else? Where in God's name were we going?*

I began to panic inside. *Why wasn't he speaking to me? Had I offended him? Was he mad at me? Was this some kind of test? Where were we going? Why hadn't he told me his plans?* My brain railed against the circumstances and exploded in questions and increased paranoia. Minutes turned to hours. In the middle of Australia you can drive forever and get nowhere. *No one knows I'm here!*

At some point, something interesting happened. The flywheel of my mind spun itself out, and everything became quiet. An enormous peace came over me. "Feels better, doesn't it?" Uncle Bob suddenly broke the silence.

My eyes burned with tears. I wasn't sure how I felt. Ashamed? Embarrassed? Relieved.

"People don't listen," he said, "they just talk and fill spaces and effort and try. Trying to be this. Trying to create that. They miss what's here now." He turned to look at me, "What's here now?" his eyes twinkling.

"Love," I responded. It wasn't love for something, it was just love. I was love. Uncle Bob was love. The infinite stretch of red dust speckled with green was love. The contrast between my habitual way of conversing to connect with others and this moment was a groundbreaking learning moment for me.

Who we are is enough. What we do, what we say—all that is just extra.

We continued driving down the dirt road for another two hours, mostly in silence. Sometimes a kangaroo would bounce past, breaking the continuous red landscape. It was the most blissful two hours of my life. Just listening to the all-that-was with all of my senses.

Finally, as the sun started to go down, we came to a place where Uncle Bob slowed down and turned off the dirt road onto an even fainter dirt road. How he knew exactly where to turn I'll never know; the entire scene looked the same to me. There was no sign, no landmark, no change in landscape that I was aware of. The Land Rover crawled over rocks, down ravines, and up to a small, flat clearing. He stopped the vehicle, turned off the engine, and got out.

"This is where these fellas will come," he said.

I looked at him quizzically. "Who?" I asked.

"The wild ones," he said. He pulled out two *swags* (a canvas bedroll-and-mat combination for camping in the bush) and several boxes filled with pots, pans, and other camping equipment. Then he instructed me to start gathering twigs for a campfire while he pulled out his guitar and a few more supplies.

As I wandered about the site looking for rocks, I noticed horse tracks, kangaroo tracks, and some huge tracks that I didn't recognize.

"Camels," he broke in. Uncle Bob often answered my unspoken questions.

The others arrived at sundown and hauled out their swags and gear. No tents—in the outback you sleep under the open sky. That night we ate canned beans and white bread. Later, Uncle Bob grabbed his guitar and we all sang songs. Then we settled into our swags and fell asleep.

A few hours later I heard a most horrifying sound. It was a loud, growling groan that I had never heard before. Uncle Bob bolted upright. "Camels!" he whispered loudly. I didn't know whether to be thrilled or terrified. I stayed awake for hours listening to their guttural calls back and forth across our campsite. The next morning when I crawled out of my swag, I saw several fresh camel footprints circling tightly around the exact spot where I had slept.

Before breakfast Uncle Bob and I walked to a billabong to watch the animals come to drink. Kangaroos, birds, lizards. And, of course, the wild horses. I learned so much by watching them.

If you were to do the same, to wander out to a clearing on a warm summer day and settle down for a few hours to watch a residing herd of horses mingle there, you would learn a lot. But you would learn nothing if you observed this herd through your preconceived lenses of what you've been taught about horses, or even what you've been taught about your own human existence. To truly learn from this magnificent teaching companion, you would need to listen differently. To actually understand how the horses organize their society, you would have to drive miles through your proverbial desert in silence until your mind stops all of its knowing and strategizing.

EQUINE CULTURE IS ORGANIZED AROUND FIVE PILLARS: SAFETY, CONNECTION, PEACE, FREEDOM, AND JOY.

At first it might appear as if not much is going on. But what you are beholding is tens of millions of years of success, elegantly fine-tuned over eons to support this particular herd in thriving not only as a family, but as an organization. Why have horses thrived for so long? There are several evolutionary reasons, but for the purposes of this book, let's focus on one of them—their culture. Now before we go on, it bears mentioning that there are hundreds, if not thousands, of books and research papers on horse behavioral sciences. What I describe here is not equine behavior but equine culture.

Based on my observation of multiple herds, wild and domestic, and a lifetime of working with horses, it is my experience that equine culture is organized around five pillars: *safety, connection, peace, freedom*, and *joy*. The leader, or the head of the family, is chosen based on their ability to maintain these pillars within the herd system. How exactly does a lead horse govern and keep those five pillars intact? Through two superpowers: *care* and *presence*.

THE LEADER IS THE ONE WHO IS NOT THE MIGHTIEST OR THE MOST DOMINEERING BUT WHO CARES THE MOST—A TRUE DEFINITION OF SERVANT LEADERSHIP.

Care is that genuine desire to attend to the needs of others. Synonymous with love, care is unconditional love with responsibility. *Presence* is the ability to be wholly here in this present moment, in this limitless sense of totality here and now. Presence enables care to be acutely responsive to the moment, in each moment. Without presence, care can be inaccurate or ill-timed. Without care, presence can remain aloof.

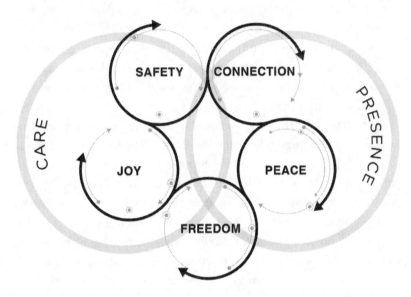

This idea of core cultural pillars is not something widely known, but one that I believe is accurate. It comes not only from decades of daily engagement with horses, but through the lens of connection that I was taught by Kabada and later Uncle Bob.

Most of us imagine a herd of horses led by a brutish, overbearing stallion using command and control tactics to rule his harem of mares. In fact, horse bands are governed by quite the opposite. The leadership position is usually assumed by a mare or a team of mares. In domestic settings, where stallions are kept separate from the herd, leadership is sometimes assumed by a quiet, caring gelding (a castrated male) in the absence of mares. The leader is the one who is not the mightiest or the most domineering but who cares the most—a true definition of servant leadership.

I want to assert that this is not about romanticizing horses; the horse culture is in no way infallible or idyllic. Like people and societies, every horse and herd is different. There are herds led by obnoxious dictators and horses too traumatized to connect. But their cultural premise remains, especially within healthy environments, and it teaches us to redefine how we think about systemic well-being and about the words *leader* and *leadership*. Most people associate those words with the business, military, or political arenas. But this is because we are culturally conditioned to narrowly define the act of leading within domination concepts: being on top, being the boss, being in control, and holding power over others. We were taught these concepts by a dominance system and belief structure, and not by true leadership itself.

In fact, the horse herd shows us that leadership is about love, connection, caring for the whole, service, and well-being. It is not a *power over*, but a *power with* dynamic. Through this expanded—and altogether more accurate—definition of leader, you may recognize that you have this innate capacity within your family, your community, your relationships, and your own selfhood—therefore, you are a leader.

When I refer to leadership throughout the entirety of this book, I deliberately use it in this more enlightened and expanded sense. I am writing about your position of power in your own life, whether you be a partner, a mother, an artist, a social worker, a soldier, an entrepreneur, or a CEO.

Today we suffer a crisis in leadership across all sectors. Absent any evidence-based definition of what leadership truly is, and operating under an assumed dominance belief-structure, throughout history we've appointed and elected leaders who are not actually leaders at all. It's no wonder we find ourselves in the current state of affairs. In fact, if we tossed these so-called leaders into a herd of wild horses, chances are the mares would quickly and fiercely send them away until they could behave.

Like our colorful, badly-behaving leaders in the public arena, gladiator stallions have received lots of attention because they are flamboyant and dramatic. Human leadership qualities have been attributed to their dominant and brutish ways. But showy stallions are not the leaders of the herd. They have a specific role to play in specific circumstances, but it's not in overseeing daily governance. In fact, the lead mare or mares will see to it that a delinquent stallion is exiled from the herd until he can participate inside the clan with good manners.

Through this elegant ecosystem of safety, peace, connection, freedom, and joy—maintained by care and presence—a dynamic democracy ensues. The other herd members are constantly, moment by moment, testing their leader's ability—does she still care? Is she still present? If for some reason, due to illness, wounding, or age, she should show up less than present or not able to care, a new leader would take her place. But not with a clashing of hooves and gnashing of teeth. Instead, with an acceptance of giving and receiving care. Out of care for the outgoing leadership (who now needs care), and care for the whole herd, a new horse assumes authority.

Let's pause here. Imagine—just for a moment—if we were to select our leaders based on their ability to be caring and profoundly present, to serve safety, connection, peace, freedom, and joy—for the whole. Imagine if our schools, our government, our financial institutions, our families, our Fortune 500s organized their cultures around these principles?

What if those of us who don't consider ourselves leaders (because we don't resonate with the *power-over* mindset) stepped into our power with more confidence because we knew our care and presence mattered? What if we stepped in to uphold safety, connection, peace, freedom, and joy? What a different world it might be.

It's not such a far reach. Take for example the prime minister of New Zealand, Jacinda Ardern, who used her debut speech to the United Nations General Assembly to directly challenge the worldview of dominance and fear. Accompanied by her three-month-old baby, she called for a different world order—one that puts kindness ahead of isolationism, rejection, and racism.

The following example reveals how this model assisted one of our clients to redefine his idea of leadership culture. Robert was a senior executive at a large conservative national organization. He came to EQUUS so that he could acquire the skills necessary to become the company's next CEO. When he arrived, he imagined he would learn how to be tougher, more intelligent, have all the answers, and effuse a commanding executive presence. After several intensive days with the horses and several months of coaching, his world was turned inside out. Make no mistake, transforming from the conventional style of leadership into a wisdom-endorsed leader is a journey that requires enormous integrity, honesty, and courage.

During one particularly poignant coaching call, a penny dropped for him. "You know," he said in relief, "all these hard-nosed yet alienating attributes I had . . . they were learned. I learned them from books and other leaders and business school. I can unlearn them. But caring? Caring is something I've known how to do since I was just a small kid. Caring is something I just am!"

In another example, Sarah, a midwife, discovered something new. "I'm not really a leader," she said as she stood next to our lead mare Artemis. Artemis, who tends to ignore almost everyone in the arena until they are ready to see that they are indeed leadership material, was gently touching Sarah all over her arms and hands.

"Really?" I queried. "Not according to Artemis, who finds you quite fascinating, especially your arms and hands . . . the tools of your trade. What does being a leader mean to you, Sarah?"

"Oh, well, leaders command other people. They are in charge of things and people. They have responsibilities." She looked down, dragging her toe in the sand. "I'm introverted. It's just me in my home office. And I don't like to impose myself on others."

"If you knew that caring was leading, would that feel like an imposition?" I nudged. We watched Artemis for a moment as she—almost on cue—pinned her ears toward our gelding Cimarron, who notoriously pushes boundaries. He wanted in on the action between the three of us—me, Sarah, and Artemis. Recognizing the ear signal, Cimarron stopped abruptly and kept a respectful distance.

"When Cimarron started to invade our quiet circle here, how did that feel?" I asked.

"I felt anxious," Sarah responded.

"And when Artemis corrected him and he stopped, how did that feel?" I continued.

"Good. I felt easy again. And, actually, now that I think about it, I felt relief." Sarah paused for a moment. Then her eyes lit up. "I . . . yes! I felt cared for!"

"That experience just now that you had—that is what real leadership feels like," I finished.

Sarah was quiet. She started to stroke Artemis's soft white fur. This kind of silence is the sound of profound change—when people are liberated from the tyranny of ill-conceived concepts and ideologies.

"When you bring a child into the world through your expertise and confidence, is that not leading the child into a safe transition?" I asked.

Sarah smiled. "Yes! And when I wake up and know what my next right action is so that I can serve the mothers and children in my care, that is leading myself so I can lead others."

When we listen to a more ancient way of life, we may discover that those of us who are compassionate, sensitive, and gentle—what researchers coin *supertraits*—have been positioned to lead our lives, our families, and the world into a new paradigm. And those of us who thought we had to be tough, hard-nosed, and demanding to lead our organizations may discover (often with substantial relief) that we can drop that armor and lean into our intrinsic nature. Like a midwife, our leadership of care and presence can serve to birth positive things into the world.

You don't need to be a special somebody to be a leader. Care and presence is your intrinsic competence. And the world needs you—whoever you are, whatever you do—to lead a flying change.

SPIRAL POINT

JOURNAL QUESTIONS

- If you were to lead your life aligned with the seven principles of 56 million years of wisdom (*safety, connection, peace, freedom*, and *joy* ensured by *care* and *presence*), what would your life be like?

- Out of all the pillars mentioned above, are there any missing in your life or your work? Which ones? What would change if you developed them more?

EXERCISES

- Design a thriving culture for your life, your family, or your organization. Take a piece of paper and list each of the pillars: safety, connection, peace, freedom, joy, care, and presence. Leave a big space between each one. Now list under each pillar two or three applications, action steps, or practices that support that value. For example, under the pillar *safety*, you could write "We support everyone to be heard, without risk of retribution." And under *connection*, you could write "I reach out to an old friend every week." Keep your list and see what changes after reading the rest of this book.

- Spend the week noticing different power dynamics around you (in your life, but also in the media, movies, news) and discern if they indicate *power with* or *power over*.

PART II
Care

A proper community . . . is a commonwealth: a place, a resource, an economy. It answers the needs, practical as well as social and spiritual, of its members—among them the need to need one another.

WENDELL BERRY,
The Art of the Commonplace:
The Agrarian Essays of Wendell Berry[1]

Care is a misunderstood phenomenon. Many get caught in the urgency of automatic reflexive responses when trying to be of help to others. We fix, rescue, and advise. Sometimes we care for another at the expense of ourselves, or care for ourselves by manipulating another. When care is impulsive, our actions are often misattuned, and we end up applying the wrong tool for the job. We can feel spent and exhausted—or resentful.

In response, sometimes we attempt to care less. We armor, we set rigid boundaries, or we distance ourselves. We become abrupt or even aggressive. In business school we are taught to be professional and leave our heart in the parking lot.

As we'll learn in the following pages, care is an essential part of leadership. Without it, a flying lead change cannot be executed, because we cannot accurately respond to the entire system. Care is the foundation for any transformative and positive change.

What then is real care? How is it that millions of years of evolution—through tectonic shifts, environmental catastrophes, and enormous climate swings—has been carried on the shoulders of this one small word? In this part of the book we will look at two concepts—care as defined by an ancient indigenous system that encompasses more than just an individualized sense of the word, and care marked by a conservation of energy that does not cost the one who delivers it.

Chapter 3
———
Kanyini

Care in the modern context is often thought of as a linear exchange. We help another, we support a cause, we donate our time. But there is another definition of care that is primordial and less transactional. It's not linear; it's circular. It's a consistent, infinite reciprocity and responsibility as modeled and taught by the natural world.

I first learned about this sacred concept from Uncle Bob in the most banal of circumstances—a tiny and sparsely furnished flat in Balmain (a suburb in the Inner West of Sydney), our home for three days while I recorded his words. The scene was bare: Uncle Bob, a recorder, and me. He sat down on a worn-out beige easy chair in front of the microphone, sinking deep into the accommodating seat cushion. I sat in front of him, cross-legged on the floor.

I suddenly realized my ambivalence in recording his words. I felt like an imposter. Naming my concern, I paused before turning on the microphone. "Is it okay for white people to learn and share your people's wisdom?" I asked.

"It is time for the *I* to give way to the *we*. The time of people saying it's *my* wisdom, not *yours*, is over," he responded. "Many of my people are too broken and too traumatized to carry on the teaching. It's not your skin color that determines if you can hear these teachings, it's your heart." He pressed his fist on my chest. "You have an aboriginal heart. You will share these words with others who have the same heart." He paused for a long time, seeming to consider the gravity of what he was saying. "I get criticized for this thinking," he said. "You too will be criticized for sharing our teachings. You will be accused of stealing. But anything that works for good should happen," he responded. "If learning our spirituality works for the good, then it must be done. Some things simply cannot be shared and so I won't. Anyway, there is a root to all spiritual systems that's all the same."

It seemed the entire universe was pouring itself into the small space between us in that tiny, insignificant living room. "Talk to me about love," I said, "and connection, and . . . well, *care*." I switched on the microphone and he began.

Uncle Bob's perspective on these topics comes from his people—the Keepers of Uluru, the Yankunytjatjara and Pitjantjatjara nations who, as a 60,000 year-old-culture, carry the most ancient human perspective on earth.

According to Uncle Bob, in order to understand the truest sense of care, one must first understand the connection that binds all of us together so we know just who it is we are caring for. We have to open ourselves to what is mysteriously known as *The Dreaming*. Trying to define The Dreaming is like trying to define God or consciousness. When pressed, Uncle Bob said it succinctly: The Dreaming is the creative presence of all that is—past, present, and future.

"The plants, land, animals, rocks, trees, mountains vibrate with The Dreaming," he said. "Therefore they are the real teachers and they communicate these truths with us. The Aboriginals are the translators of that. If you want to know what care really is, you must listen to the answer with your solar plexus, your gut . . . and your head, heart, eyes, ears . . . to hear what these teachers have to say. They are the ones that know."

Through The Dreaming, we are all connected. It is the *livingness*—the beingness—that connects us. This might be easy to get your head around with regard to animals and even plants. But The Dreaming understanding of what it means to be animate diverges from the list of attributes of living beings we learned in biology class. In Aboriginal culture, the rocks are animate, as are clouds, rivers, and mountains. Uncle Bob would say things like, "Go see that fella there," pointing to a bush, or "Let's say hello to our sisters," looking up at the stars.

The livingness binds us in kinship, literally, to all elements: water, fire, air, and earth. The more you hear about The Dreaming, the more it sounds like the latest quantum physics research. Or perhaps it's the other way around. The more we peer into the nature of reality from either side of the coin, spiritual or scientific, the more they come together.

As soon as scientists began smashing electrons and other particles in enormous accelerators, they quickly realized the foundations of the physical world weren't physical at all—that everything is energy. As we bend our minds from string theory, to entanglement theory, to the theory of relativity, and from one theory of spacetime to the other, we finally come to that mysteriously paradoxical place where time is and isn't, things are and aren't, where all is one yet nothing exists—the place that Aboriginals elegantly call The Dreaming. Here—whether you call it energy, life force, or beingness—we are all the same.

When we recognize our kinship with all of life through whichever lens most resonates with us—scientific or spiritual—then we have a taste of an unconditional love. We are profoundly connected, without conditions. In the same way that we are responsible for our own body—the food we eat, the exercise we embody, the sunscreen we put on our skin—we are responsible for all the other parts of ourselves in the world. In the Yankunytjatjara language, this notion of unconditional love, born of the recognition of our connection with all things, and therefore our responsibility to all things, is called *Kanyini*.

"It is our responsibility—not just Aboriginals' but everyone's—to live by what my people call the Kanyini principle," said Uncle Bob. "There's such a huge family you're responsible for, and who you belong to, because they see you as belonging to them as well. And when I say family, I mean all beings, not just human beings."

Kanyini helps us to understand a more profound notion of caring beyond just being helpful or kind. Care from a Kanyini point of view comes from a sense of oneness and connectedness, as well as a responsibility to the other, because we are part of an interrelated whole. Responsibility can take gentle forms, but can also be fierce, challenging, confronting, and direct. This is the part of care that is less understood by humans.

Horses model Kanyini powerfully. They care from a unified perspective much larger and broader than our own—one that has the ability to hold extremes without tension—and act from a more informed holistic position. The culture of the horse is not always comfortable for humans. Horses can have highly charged polarities within paradoxes. Unlike the human mind's dualism that separates the world into good–bad, right–wrong, either–or, this–or–that, horses teach *both-and*. An underlying unity is revealed in their herd dynamics. They respond in the moment to what is arising, aligned with the principles of safety, connection, peace, freedom, and joy, as created by care for the whole (system, herd, family, etc).

For the horse, care in one moment could look like standing protectively in front of another horse, so that a threat (such as an abusive human) cannot approach. In another moment, care is expressed through gentle mutual grooming and muzzling. And care in the next moment can look like an alpha mare harshly, even violently, exiling a misbehaving yearling colt from the herd, leaving him to fend for himself, vulnerable to predators, completely isolated from the others. Care serves the whole, rather than individual needs or preferences. You could say that horses seem to have the ability to act upon a bigger picture and in so doing seem to act outside of themselves, i.e., outside of their own self-interest. This can be confronting to us humans who may not understand a sudden and harsh equine response.

Our horse Cimarron, a gaily spotted leopard Appaloosa, had a tough introduction to our closely bonded herd when he first arrived. For some reason, Cimarron had not learned the proper social etiquette of herd culture. Many domesticated horses are denied this important education because they live in stalls or in environments that are absent the strict tutelage of mares—the disciplinarians of the herd.

Cimarron had no sense of boundaries. He was excited to make new friends, but his enthusiasm caused him to approach others without sensing their personal space. He'd rush up to each horse eagerly only to be met with kicks and bites. He'd try to share food with another and find himself chased away to the far corner of the paddock.

Most horses learn quickly the social norms, and as soon as that happens they are welcomed into the herd. Not Cimarron. If Cimarron is anything, he is persistent. For months he continued to invade boundaries, and the corrections from the others became more intense and severe. At one point there were as many bite marks on his body as spots.

This scenario can be difficult for humans to understand and accept, especially when they see Cimarron covered in bite marks and not making any friends. But from a larger point of view, we can see that Cimarron's inability to understand space and boundaries makes him a risk to the herd and himself. Space (as we'll learn in a subsequent chapter) allows the horses to respond to danger in a fluid manner without crashing into each other. Boundaries allow for the horses to have order and discern what can come close and what cannot. The herd's response was actually care in action—care for the whole, and care for Cimarron.

It was becoming apparent that Cimarron was not learning from the others. He was not only clueless about equine social conduct, but also clueless about how to learn from his fellow equines! Then I had an idea. Given that he had spent most of his life in the company of humans, I thought I'd step in as his *tutor mare*. Each day I would take him into the arena and teach him about boundaries. I would stand over a bowl of grain and not let him have any. If he stepped forward uninvited, he was promptly corrected. If he could manage a few moments of self-restraint, I praised him. I would move into his space and teach him to give way. Then I would invite him into my space, playing with varying degrees of approach. I continued praising each time he recognized and respected the faintest sense of a boundary.

At the end of each session, I would take him back to his paddock of friends. Instead of releasing him, triggering his unchecked enthusiasm to return to the herd and hijacking his newly learned spatial skills, I walked him calmly to the other horses, modelling how to approach them sensitively to their spatial preferences. Cimarron felt—probably for the first time in his life—the silent acceptance from the other horses.

Within just a few days Cimarron had the space-boundary thing nailed. He also learned that he too could ask for space and even play with space. In time he became such a space aficionado that he taught the other horses how to playfully dance with space and boundaries together. You can now watch Cimarron and his fellow horses outrageously colliding, twirling, galloping, and wrestling inside hours of hilarious and delightful entertainment.

We humans can get all tied up into knots when we are trying to care. It's hard to find that position outside of ourselves. The ways of Kanyini have not been taught to us. We're not sure what to do with the teenager who continuously takes drugs and crashes the family car. We hand-wring about the partner who gambles, or the boss who betrays our trust. Or we helicopter-parent our kids into bubble-wrapped oblivion, rendering them incapable of independence.

The Kanyini Care Diagram[1]

Diagram inspired by Kim Scott's Radical Candor framework and her book *Radical Candor: Be a Kick-Ass Boss Without Losing Your Humanity*, where she encourages readers to "care personally" and "challenge directly."

Let's walk through the quadrants presented in the diagram. In the upper left-hand corner, we see a behavior that is informed by care, but it's not care for the whole. Instead, it's care of someone's feelings. Here we caretake by withholding challenge so as not to hurt the person. In the lower left-hand corner, we are merely protecting our own feelings and withhold challenging another because we fear for how we might be hurt or punished, or maybe we just want to be liked. The lower right quadrant is simply not caring at all, yet able to challenge. However, when we do so, we do it aggressively. And finally, the upper right-hand quadrant—the

CARE LEVERAGES THE AUTHORITY TO CHALLENGE OTHERS. WITHOUT CARE, CHALLENGE IS DESTRUCTIVE. YET WITHOUT CHALLENGE, CARE IS POWERLESS.

Kanyini quadrant—where we care deeply and for the whole (system, family, team, organization). Our care for the other grants us the authority to act out of self and therefore act directly, speak clearly and candidly, and challenge mindfully, thus serving the whole. Optimally, we act out of this quadrant as much as possible.

One of our clients learned about care the hard way. Julie was a high-ranking official for the state. She worked to unify her team of senior leaders by engaging EQUUS to facilitate an ongoing peer group circle—named Wisdom Circle—that met monthly at their offices. Inside the Wisdom Circle, they incorporated the principles of herd organization and upheld the principles of safety, connection, peace, freedom, and joy through care and presence. This created a closely bonded team of empowered collaborators. As the Wisdom Circle widened, the principles that held them together began to infuse the rest of the organization. The whole department began to perform better and report much higher work satisfaction.

Then the governor asked Julie to appoint someone (Barbara) to an important position who had no clue about navigating the conscious culture now embedded within the team. Wanting to please the governor, Julie acted hastily and agreed, even though, much like Cimarron, Barbara invaded space, manipulated boundaries, was divisive, and, well, badly behaved. But unlike Cimarron, Barbara did not receive the disciplinary kicks and bites from the team or the alpha mare.

In her stress, Julie forgot how to be a leader and devolved into pleasing. She even manipulated the team (in the guise of care) into ignoring her unskillfulness and instead emphasized making Barbara feel welcome. This is not care. This is not Kanyini. It's fear masked as care. The more Julie and her team contorted themselves to accommodate Barbara, the more Barbara acted out. In the end, the leadership team ruptured.

In this world of numbing out and instant gratification, we humans tend to lack the capacity to bear the discomfort resulting from acting outside of self to serve the whole. So we do what's easy instead of what's right. In Julie's case, she let her discomfort around disciplining Barbara prevent her from truly leading her team and her organization. She cared more for her own emotional safety than for her team—operating from the lower left-hand quadrant of the model. Kanyini invites us to befriend discomfort. True care does not always feel comfortable. We sometimes have to feel temporary friction, pain, or loss around an individual (or our individual sense of self) to serve the greater good. Here's the thing: care leverages the authority to challenge others. Without care, challenge is destructive. Yet without challenge, care is powerless.

When we function outside of self, we have the uncommon ability to not only see the whole system but see past, present, and future, and act accordingly. In other words, we are informed by The Dreaming. We are practicing Kanyini—unconditional love with responsibility.

Is there a dysfunctional friendship that no longer belongs in your circle? Is there a behavior of a family member that is no longer acceptable? Does someone in your life need to be challenged? Or, conversely, is there an action required of you, albeit uncomfortable, that would align you more with the whole—an apology perhaps, or being accountable for something? Are you open to being challenged?

Horses and nature remind us to live in balance, to walk that line between harshness and gentleness, between almost-unbearable lightness and tragedy. These are not polarities; they are complementaries that dance together in the play of Kanyini.

SPIRAL POINT

JOURNAL QUESTIONS

- Is there a person or people in your life whom you care for but need to challenge or set a boundary with?

- Think of someone in your life who demonstrated care with responsibility. They were able to care and at the same time be clear, direct, and candid with you. How did they impact you?

EXERCISES

- Draw a Kanyini Care Diagram like the one earlier in this chapter. Now spend the week charting yourself on the diagram. Where do you habitually land?

- Challenge yourself to operate from the Kanyini quadrant of the diagram more often. What practices or behaviors do you need to shift to do that?

Chapter 4

Conservation of Energy

C are should not cost you. It should not endlessly exhaust us to raise a family, create a start-up, or tend to those in need. But somewhere along the line we learned that care meant expending our energies indiscriminately until we arrive at the end of the day collapsed in front of our televisions, drink in hand.

Everything we do takes energy. To answer the phone takes energy. To have lunch with a friend takes energy. To avoid a difficult but necessary conversation takes energy. Nature designs all living things to conserve energy as much as possible, so that when energy is actually needed (in a horse's case, to escape the lion, for example) we have it in reserve. In the modern pace of artificial emergency, humans unnecessarily expend energy all the time. Everything feels urgent and critical. What if we lived more deliberately, expended energy only specifically and only when truly required?

Horses reveal a surprising counter move to our misguided idea of care, and it has to do with the amount of energy expended and conserved in any given moment. In fact, in the herd the one who cares the most is not only the leader but the one who moves the least and expends the least energy.

A folding chair lies on its side by our horse paddocks. Some days, instead of working the horses, I'll grab the chair, open the paddock gate, and carry it into the shade of the juniper trees, or if it's cool, out in a sunny clearing. There I'll unfold the chair and park myself for up to an hour. Often I'm ignored, except for our barn cat Lizzie who takes the opportunity for some lap time. Sometimes I'll end up with a pile of horses around me, nuzzling me. But the purpose of my visit is not for attention. I simply want to better learn the silent language of horses.

> LEARNING THE DIFFERENCE BETWEEN CARE AND CARETAKING LIBERATES US TO CARE POWERFULLY IN A WAY THAT DOES NOT COST US.

The best teacher on care is our lead horse Artemis. She's usually standing in the shade of a piñon tree, a little separate from the rest, her eyes gently closing, her hind hoof resting at an angle to the ground. Artemis is modeling care in action.

"She's not doing anything," remarked Karen, a mother of two teenage boys when she first met the mare.

Karen and her sons came to EQUUS to find their way back to each other. "I want to bring my boys to the horses so that we can reconnect again," she wrote in her email. "The boys are underperforming in school, and my youngest, I fear, is becoming depressed." When they arrived at Thunderbird Ridge, Karen burst out of the car a little too enthusiastically; the boys snailed behind her, staring at the ground.

Karen was strung tightly in that "supermom" vibe that's epidemic to American mothers. It was fascinating to watch their dynamic. Her eyes were wide, she spoke fast, and she overcompensated for her boys' disengagement. The more she pressed them into conversing with us, the more they pulled back. "Say hello to Scott and Kelly," she urged briskly, literally maneuvering their little bodies to face us.

Overfunctioning, caretaking, rescuing, and fixing are a recipe for disaster in any system, familial or organizational. Absent any anciently informed teaching about what true care is, we default into these other habits. Learning the difference between care and caretaking liberates us to care powerfully in a way that does not cost us.

In my work with clients, I often use indigenous teaching stories or poetry to explore a theme. One of my favorite tales I first heard from a colleague is a fiercely instructive teaching story called "The Origin of Different Water Animals" from Nagaland, India.[1] It offers strong medicine for a society addicted to caretaking.

The *Naga* are a group of tribes living in the northeastern corner of India and northwestern Myanmar. Nagaland is a place of stunning beauty. Sitting on the eastern side of the Himalayas, the mountainous terrain is rugged and lined in a patchwork of villages where life continues as it has for centuries. A warrior culture, the most senior Naga elders are covered with tattoos, face and body signifying their conquests. Naga people speak over eighty-nine different languages and dialects, and they have a strong storytelling tradition.

As earlier, this story begins with *Once, long ago . . .*

a crab, a frog, a shrimp, and a minnow were friends. All four were females and they worked together well. Each helped the others by doing what she could do best. Each day at dinnertime they arranged a fine meal and ate together. Like humans, these animals grew rice. They worked as a group in one another's fields, thus making the work more enjoyable due to the company. The four took turns cooking. The one whose turn it was to cook would leave the field early and go home to prepare dinner. When it was ready she would call her friends from the fields, asking them to join her.

After a while it was agreed that the crab's cooking was the best. So they asked the crab if she would cook every day. She would be delighted to, she said, and thereafter this was her job. One day, there was no meat available to make a decent meal. So the crab took off one of her own legs and added it to the vegetables. When the meal was ready she called her friends as usual. They thought the meal was especially delicious that day and helped themselves to extra portions.

They praised crab for sacrificing her leg and making such a wonderful meal, even in a time of want.

The crab was so pleased with the praise she received from her friends that she continued to remove one after another of her legs each day. She put each leg into the curry until only the stump of her body remained. Each day the group praised her again for her cooking and urged her to continue in her role as chef. She gladly accepted, because their praise warmed her heart.

One day, while the group of three friends was working in the field they realized it was already past time for their midday meal. Still they waited patiently for the crab to call them to dinner. But there was no call. Eventually they decided to go home anyway. But the crab was not at the house. The friends called for her but there was no answer. They decided that she must have returned to the river to bathe or perhaps grow new legs. They were hungry and so they decided to eat without waiting for her. It was already quite late. As they opened the curry pot to serve their food, there was the crab's body right in the middle of the curry, flavoring the whole dish with her tasty meat.

Seeing the sacrifice the crab had made of herself, the other three animals all started to laugh. They laughed and laughed until they couldn't stand up straight. They laughed until they rolled around on the floor. They laughed until evening, when they finally stopped from sheer exhaustion. When the frog tried to get up, however, she could no longer stand erect. Her back had become permanently bent at the base of the spine from laughing so hard. The fish's neck had become so swollen that it no longer had the graceful curves it used to have. Now it was stiff and straight.

The shrimp could no longer walk forward, but only backward as she had been doing during her fit of laughter. Unable to continue their work in the fields, all these animals took to the water. And that is where we find them today.

Let's just pause here for just a moment. How does this story affect you? What gets triggered? Where do you feel emotional? What shuts down? Where do you get defensive or judgmental?

I read Karen and her boys this story before we went in to work with the horses. Karen's face turned ashen. The boys, too, were strongly impacted. Such is the work of a strong medicine story.

"I'm the crab," Karen said. "I'm always giving away pieces of myself thinking I'm taking good care of everyone."

"Well, I think the frog, the minnow, and the shrimp were jerks," her youngest son Sam weighed in. "They laughed at her death, and all she was doing was feeding them."

"Yeah, but the crab was so stupid," countered Ely, her oldest.

"Why didn't the shrimp, the minnow, and the frog say something to the crab when she started removing parts of her body? Why didn't they take care of her?" retorted Sam emphatically.

Therein lay the internal unconscious dialogue of this family's dynamic. The beauty of these stories is that they actively work within each person differently. Traditional stories, from any culture around the world, are active, living entities that move inside our psyche and encourage a form of neural rewiring.

We walked out to the horses. Artemis was standing just a little separate from the rest, looking out over the arena fence with her ears pricked forward. The other horses were playing and romping around. I spoke to the family about how the leader of the horse herd is the one who cares the most.

"To care, you have to be truly present, right? Who do you think is the most present?" I asked, nodding toward the arena filled with horses.

The family was silent. "Who do you think would notice the lion first?" I reframed.

Sam was quick. "Artemis," he said. "She's really got her attention focused on something in the trees. The others are just, well, distracted with their own thing."

The family of three roamed around the arena, meeting each horse one by one. Cimarron, our infamous boundary pusher, was naturally all over them. At first glance this seemed congenial. He rubbed his face all over Karen's coat, leaving her covered in white and black hair.

"He likes me," she said. I didn't reply.

Cimarron followed them closely as they approached Artemis. He tried wedging himself between the family and her. The family accommodated and let Cimarron have his way, but Artemis instantly responded with pinned ears. He ignored her, so she tossed her head. He ignored her even more. In a flash, she leapt at Cimarron with teeth bared. He whirled away, leaving the family and Artemis to enjoy the space together in peace. Artemis exhaled and closed her eyes. For some time the family stood with her in silence, while the other horses, including Cimarron, continued to play at the other end of the arena.

Karen started to notice the differences between how she cared for her boys and how Artemis cared for the herd. "If I were the mare in this herd, I'd be running around trying to make all the horses calm down. I'd be trying to control everything."

The boys giggled. "Yeah," Ely joked elbowing his mother, "you'd be tearing off all your crab legs!"

"And anyways, what good did it do any of those water animals?" said Sam. "The crab died. And the others guys just ended up in the water all messed up."

Karen exhaled—half in defeat, half in relief. "Frankly, I'm exhausted most days. But watching Artemis . . . she just made a small efficient correction, then settled herself back into just being. It was all really easy. And she spends way more of her time just being than doing."

"And how did that feel, to be cared for in that way . . . that she quickly and succinctly requested Cimarron to give you all space and then settled into just being with you?" I asked.

"It felt amazing," said Ely. "It felt so peaceful."

"Yeah, it did," added Sam. "Mom . . . " he hesitated, "sometimes all

I want is to *just be* with you. I don't want to be all perfect and doing things all the time."

Artemis models care by what she doesn't do—caretake, run around, and micromanage everything. She is in much more of a state of being than doing. By her quiet presence, she regulates (keeps calm) her nervous system, which in turn positively influences and regulates the nervous system of the whole herd. Nervous systems of all creatures (including ours) are designed to feel and influence other nervous systems. By standing quietly in a peaceful state, she manages the herd's well-being in a powerful way by creating a field of ease.

Start to notice your internal state when you are taking care of another. Are you tense, moving fast, feeling rigid inside? It is probably a sign that you are caretaking instead of truly caring. When we caretake, we are wasting energy, running around the arena of our lives trying to control the romping horses. Unwittingly, when we care for others in that way, we are holding them small, imagining they are not capable to learn their own lessons or do what is required. We disempower them rather than empower them. Plus, we add stress waves to the nervous system of the environment, creating more dis-ease and tension for everyone involved.

The more you practice caring like Artemis, the more love, spaciousness, ease, and presence will enter your life. You will have more energy, you will truly care better, and you'll empower others to do the same.

SPIRAL POINT

JOURNAL QUESTIONS

- What impact did the crab story have on you? Write about it.

- What did you learn about care from Artemis? How does that differ from how you were taught about leadership in the human domain? If you lead your family, your life, your team, or your venture like Artemis leads, what would change?

EXERCISES

- When waking up from the trance of caretaking and learning new habits of true care, it's important to start with small, doable steps. Start with minor scenarios and flex those new caring muscles using light weights. For example, notice a moment where you are tense about a partner's relationship with their sibling and you want to caretake by making a suggestion to them. Pause. Notice the cost to you—the crab leg tossed in the pot in the form of tension and anxiety, as well as how it takes you away from being present in the moment. Instead, simply do nothing and stay quietly, calmly present.

- Write one small, practical action step that you can take in the next seven days that would assist you to conserve your energy more. Whatever it is, commit to doing it.

PART III
Presence

If you bring a certain kind of open, moment-to-moment, nonjudgmental awareness to what you're attending to, you'll begin to develop a more penetrative awareness that sees beyond the surface of what's going on in your field of awareness. This is mindfulness. Mindfulness makes it possible to see connections that may not have been visible before.

JON KABAT-ZINN,
as quoted in *Presence: An Exploration of Profound Change in People, Organizations, and Society*[1]

Presence is not about our physicality, nor is it about time (as in *the present moment*). Though accessed through this moment, true presence is alive and dynamic and stretches across time and space. Presence is a state of being. We meet the here and now with vulnerability, and we open our senses to what is emerging—and what we can influence—from this illuminated state.

Presence is the foundational underpinning of all mastery, skill, and innovation. When we engage in the world without deliberate presence, we are reacting to the moment from a past perspective or an imagined future. We are shadowboxing. Presence lifts us out of the boxing ring and into the possibility of responding to what is real. In this section we explore three aspects of presence as informed by nature-based wisdom: beingness, emergence, and persistence. You will learn not only how to be more present, but more importantly how to be *in presence*, and how to lean into sensing the innovative emergent future from that place of presence. And you will learn one of the most powerful ways presence impacts change—through subtle yet consistent perseverance. Presence gathers and potentiates your greatest strengths for a flying lead change.

Chapter 5

Beingness

On a sweltering South Indian afternoon in July of 1896, a teenager named Venkataraman was sitting on the floor of his uncle's house. Suddenly and inexplicably he was overcome by an acute fear of death. So he decided right there and then to see what it was like to be dead. He lay down on the floor, froze rigor mortis–like, and explored the experience fully.

Decades later, he narrated his inquiry, "But with the death of this body, am I dead? Is the body 'I'? I am spirit transcending the body. The body dies but the spirit that transcends it cannot be touched by death."[1]

Though he never sought devotees and seldom spoke, people from around the world gathered around him because his presence was so powerful. Just sitting near him would give people a taste of pure beingness. He became known as Ramana Maharshi, one of the most celebrated saints in history, and he introduced the modern world to a practice called *self-inquiry*. His spiritual teacher was a silent mountain named Arunachala.[2]

Ramana advised practitioners to put their attention on the inner feeling of *I*.[3] This practice of awareness is a gentle technique that bypasses the usual repressive methods of controlling the mind. It is not an exercise in concentration, nor does it aim at suppressing thoughts; it merely invokes awareness of the source from which thought springs. "Do not meditate—be," coached Ramana. "Be as you are."[4]

Ramana mostly taught through silence. Words, he mused, merely point us in a direction; silence gives us a sense of pure awareness, this *being as we are*—a powerful way to live and work. Nature, too, teaches through silence and invites us every moment to simply *be* as a foundational underpinning to all that we *do*. If we deliberately put our attention and energy on beingness throughout the day, our doing is infused with ease, delight, wisdom, and joy. Beingness connects us to our deepest selves, and it tethers us to all that which exists. If we want to create a life of safety, connection, peace, joy, and freedom, beingness is the keystone.

> IF WE DELIBERATELY PUT OUR ATTENTION AND ENERGY ON BEINGNESS THROUGHOUT THE DAY, OUR DOING IS INFUSED WITH EASE, DELIGHT, WISDOM, AND JOY.

If you spend time with a herd of horses, you'll experience for yourself how beingness pervades the space that they live inside. What appears as hanging about doing nothing is actually their active engagement and enjoyment of beingness—as if they are bathing in a field of connection. Why? Not only because it feels good, but because we are designed by nature—all of us—to be present.

After spending the morning with our herd, my wonderful editor Buzzy Jackson told me, "The word that comes to mind when I'm with them is *immanence*." I later looked up the exquisitely perfect term. Immanence holds that the divine encompasses or is manifested in the material world—a felt sense of divine presence here on earth. Immanence is usually applied in various faiths to suggest that the spiritual world permeates the mundane. It is often contrasted with theories of transcendence, in which the divine is seen to be outside the material world.

Clinical professor of psychiatry at the UCLA School of Medicine, founding co-director of the Mindful Awareness Research Center, and prolific author Dan Siegel asserts that by cultivating your capacity to be present in this way, you are "integrating your brain—growing the linkages among its different regions, strengthening the brain's ability to regulate things such as emotion, attention, thought, and behavior, learning to live a life with more flexibility and freedom."[5] Not only does integrating your brain in this way change the health of our body and slow aging, but it increases kindness and compassion, reduces stress, and increases our sense of belonging, meaning, and purpose, writes Siegel.[6]

Self-inquiry or "being in beingness," Ramana said, should not be regarded as a meditation practice that takes place at certain hours and in certain positions; it should continue throughout one's waking hours, irrespective of what one is doing.[7] He saw no conflict between working and self-inquiry, and he maintained that with a little practice it could be done under any circumstances.

Luckily, we don't have to travel all the way to India and sit with a saint to get the experience of pure awareness. We can sit in nature. We can hang with some horses. We can do exactly what young Venkataraman was compelled to do after his awakening. Rather than sit with a spiritual teacher, he sat with a mountain.

Uncle Bob once told me a story about a British man who flew all the way to the center of Australia to learn from one of Uncle Bob's people's elders. It was the 1960s, around the time countless Westerners started to flock around Indian saints. Apparently the man braved plane, bus, and dusty Range Rover across the wild and scorched Australian bush to find the elder.

"I want to be your spiritual student," he proclaimed to the elder once he finally found him.

The elder ignored him for many days. The man persisted. "Please, I'll do anything," he said.

The elder paused, glared at him for a long time through his heavy brow, and finally spoke. "See that tree there down thatta way?" he said, nodding down the long stretch of red sand, across the bush to one spare tree in the distance.

"Yes," answered the British man, a little too eagerly.

"Sit there. Do not move. I'll send for you when it is time," instructed the elder.

The man gathered his backpack and canteen, and went to sit under the tree. Hours passed. Evening came. Night passed. Days passed. The elder never sent for the man.

Finally, the man got up, defeated and indignant. He marched up to the camp and threw down his hat in the dust in front of the circle of people sitting together, the elder amongst them.

"Where have you been?" he fumed. "I've been sitting at that bloody tree for literally days!"

No one looked up, except the elder, who stared in the man's eyes for what seemed a decade. "Did you not listen?" he queried. "That fella (meaning the tree) taught you everything you needed to know." And with that he turned his back on the man.

"What happened to the man?" I asked Uncle Bob, like a child after a bedtime story.

"Who knows," Uncle Bob chuckled.

Artemis is a similar stern governess. When Artemis pins her ears at a client as they eagerly pet her, they can feel rejected. I encourage them to notice how she did not walk away, but instead remained quietly alongside them. "What is she trying to impart to you? Every time you reach to pet her, she pins her ears. But every time you settle near her, just being, she relaxes."

What she is teaching, with the mere pin of her ears, is that being-ness is enough. You are enough. All that doing and petting just gets in the way of presence. Your simple yet profound beingness is more important than you may realize.

SPIRAL POINT

JOURNAL QUESTIONS

- How much time do you spend just being? What might change in your life if you spent a bit more time in beingness?

- Who are you? Keep asking yourself the question and journaling your answers, going further and further into the inquiry.

EXERCISES

- Instead of meditating, pause and take a few moments throughout the day to just be. What is that like?

- How do you live according to the tree, the horse, the mountain, a Brahmin saint? All you need do is distinguish *being something* from *just being*, and discern *awareness* from that which you are *aware of*. Even in this moment, you are aware of the book in your hands and the words in front of you. Now inquire who (or what) is aware.

Chapter 6

Emergence

Presence is dynamic. It is not just a solid point in time, out of time. It has depth and capacity; it is the seed in which are latent, infinite possibilities. The term *emergence* describes that expectant potential. And when one is truly present, so present that there is even a departure from identifying as a *someone*, then a creative potent force—and our co-creation with it—begins to reveal itself. This is the home of intuition and the birthplace of innovation.

"But I can't just stare at my belly button all day. I've got things to do." Ben was a fast-moving entrepreneur who came to EQUUS to cultivate his intuition. We were sitting quietly among the herd enjoying just being. He didn't actually come out and say it, but you could almost see the speech bubble above his head that said, "Enough of this woo-woo, New Age, touchy-feely stuff. Time's up." Scott and I hear this a lot. Who has time for presence? Scott's retort is often that presence is one of the most ancient of practices, hardly New Age. Presence informs doing. Without presence, we are just reacting. We are just pure mechanistic reflex, wasting energy, repeating old patterns. Presence isn't some option on the spiritual menu; it's life. And since Ben was coming to us specifically to learn how to trust and build his intuition, he was getting a big dose of *be here now*.

This is where things get really interesting. If you are willing to commit to being present, to being in the state of beingness or awareness as a primary fidelity, a whole amazing world of possibility and probability reveals itself to you. Your intuition sharpens and a prescience emerges. You can sense the future before it arrives. Does this sound like sorcery? It's not. It's as practical and everyday as driving your car. If, that is, you are willing to slow down.

If Ben was going to cultivate his ability to know things immediately, without the crutch of reasoning, he would have to step away from his habit of speed and an idea of his self as something defined by doing and spend more time in the moment. After an hour or so, when I sensed his tight grip on mental urgency soften, I invited him to watch the horses carefully.

"Now that you are being really present . . . from here, with your awareness, lean into what is about to emerge for each horse," I said. Ben looked at me quizzically. "Sense when one is about to shift their weight, or nudge a fly, or . . . " I could already tell Ben was tuning into what we call the *field of emergent possibility*. It's palpable when someone is working from this place.

Ben sat quietly on the ground, breathing slowly, watching. Within minutes he was smiling broadly. "I can see it! I can sense when something is about to happen, and it does!" He was practically hopping around cross-legged. He quieted down again and continued to watch, drawn to the world that was revealing itself to him, just one microsecond ahead of the present moment.

"This is sensing the emergent future," I told him. "We often don't tune ourselves to recognizing this important nascent moment because we're moving too fast into the future or reflecting so much on the past. Seldom are we just here."

I first learned to hone this skill as a horsewoman. Tom Dorrance, one of the forefathers of fine horsemanship, would advise riders to be so present with their horses that they could sense the horse's decision to do something before they did it. That's when you respond, and not a millisecond later.

"That's a week too late," scolded one of my trainers who had once apprenticed with Tom back in the day. I was doing a simple exercise of bracing slightly on Dante's rein to get him to bend his head around and then quickly releasing the rein's pressure as an immediate reward when he did it (yielded to the pressure). But apparently my instant release to Dante's yielding was not instant enough.

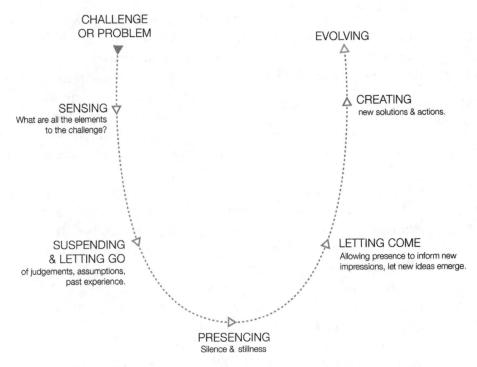

CHALLENGE
OR PROBLEM

EVOLVING

SENSING
What are all the elements
to the challenge?

CREATING
new solutions & actions.

SUSPENDING
& LETTING GO
of judgements, assumptions,
past experience.

LETTING COME
Allowing presence to inform new
impressions, let new ideas emerge.

PRESENCING
Silence & stillness

Diagram licensed by the Presencing Institute – Otto Scharmer

"Release the pressure when you sense he has *decided* to yield. Can you be that attuned? Or are you just going to hang on that rein till Christmas?" When working with exceptionally talented horse people, it's like sitting beneath a Zen master and their stick. Ouch.

Organizational change agents and authors Joseph Jaworski, Peter Senge, and Otto Scharmer created a theory around this way of sensing, and they now apply it to innovative societal change.[1] Scharmer calls it *Theory U*—the U modeling the mental trajectory taken when one senses the emergent future from the present moment.[2] At the top of the U on the left hand side is the situation as it presently is. Let's take the horses in the paddock with Ben for example. Traveling down the U is a moment of information gathering and observation. In Ben's case he would be noticing the horses standing or moving around, noticing their colors, sizes, and shapes. So far, nothing innovative here. We all look out and see our world every day. However, moving down toward the bottom of the U is where the game changes.

In most situations, particularly in problem-solving scenarios, we tend to act in a knee-jerk fashion. We see the situation, we gather information, and then we act. It's a cognitive, rational response, which is fine. However, this kind of problem-solving has an overlaying routine solution based on past experience. It results in a short-term improvement rather than a more innovative solution. To use a simple example, let's say we have a headache. Instead of pausing, we grab for the aspirin, take the pill, and move on. The problem is, if we continue with this kind of problem-solving, we'll incur more health issues as a side effect of taking aspirin every time we get a headache.

In the U scenario, instead of immediately acting, there is a different step: pausing, suspending all we think we know, and finally becoming truly present. Senge calls it *presencing*.[3] This presencing step lands us at the bottom of the U, exactly where I asked Ben to be while sitting in the paddock. It is there that the magic happens. To be at the bottom of the U, one has to let go of all assumptions, let go of doing, let go of future and past. You are, like Ramana, sitting at the foot of Arunachala. There, the universe and all its creative potential avails itself to you—represented in the upswing of the U. There, you don't act out of deduction; you act from inner feel, as informed by a greater consciousness found in presence. This is the origin of *inspiration*, a word with the etymological reference to the divine. Going back to our headache example above, when the problem is met with pausing, suspending, and presencing, we discover that our headache is a symptom of something larger in our lives—our chronic overcommitting, for example. Now we can take a more effective action than taking an aspirin—in this case, reduce our commitments.

We see parallels of Theory U in art, sports, martial arts, and science. The exceptional people in these fields appear to be accessing from someplace else than their logic. Einstein himself believed his best ideas came to him during his violin breaks, what he called *combinatory play*—allowing his mind to have a wilderness of associations, imagery, and elements reaching across boundaries of various theories and fields of thought, not as deliberate problem-solving but as unforced mental meanderings.[4] My guess is that if we pressed Einstein about the moment before he allowed the meanderings, he'd call it presence.

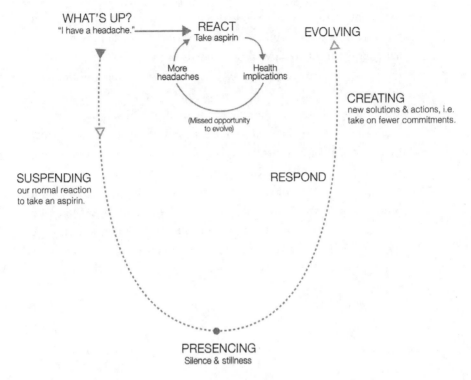

Diagram licensed by the Presencing Institute – Otto Scharmer

The masters (and true founders) of the theory of the U can of course be found in nature. Nature designs us all to be acutely aware and accurately responsive in order to thrive. In the case of the horses or any animal of prey, if they miss sensing the emergent future, they become another creature's meal. The stakes are high. Learning from their way of being teaches us to be as acutely present so that we can be optimally anticipatory and responsive to our emerging future.

When we study the arc of a 56-million-year-old system, we are not following a line that begins on the primitive side and terminates on the advanced. We are seeing the narrative of successful adaptation and evolutionary innovation through present attunement. With all the challenges upon us now as a species, we would do well to learn the nimble art form of presencing and sensing the emergent future as modeled by *Equus caballus* when they respond to every unfolding moment through being in beingness.

The next time you find yourself in a situation that requires your intelligent problem-solving or some kind of genius response, challenge yourself to slow down and drop in to that quiet state of beingness. I have found that my relationships with my children and with Scott have all benefitted from this approach. Scenarios that would ordinarily trigger me due to my own past history now unfold differently with ease and more creativity. All you need do is pause, let go, and hang out in presence for a few minutes. Then, just as Ben did, lean into the micro-next-moment with your awareness. It may appear at first in the form of vague images or impressions. Stay with them and allow the hints of possibility to emerge. And just like one of those cool autostereograms, where the three-dimensional image slowly appears out of the colorful chaos when you settle your gaze, so will your intuition reveal the right solution.

SPIRAL POINT

JOURNAL QUESTIONS

- How did this chapter impact you? What are your reflections on problem-solving and leaning into the emergent future to see more possibilities?

- What are some areas in your life that would benefit from this kind of presence and attention? What might change if, inside these areas, you allowed the process of pausing, being present, and allowing for innovative seeing to emerge?

EXERCISES

- Do the U: think of an issue, challenge, or problem that you would like to practice presencing with. Write about it at length—all the issues and details associated with it. Next, put your paper aside and close your eyes, allowing all of your preconceived ideas about the issue to just settle and quiet. Just see it for what it is—not good, not bad. Next, exhale, close your eyes, and just allow yourself to be present, calm, and still inside. Do this for about five minutes. Then with eyes still closed, allow for the subconscious and the collective life force around you to filter through. At first you may have just images, impressions, words. Let them in. Open your eyes and on a fresh sheet of paper draw, write, diagram all the impressions that came your way. It's okay if they don't seem to make sense—this is the raw material of the emergent possible future. Spend some time with it and now write any thoughts, ideas, or actions that start to congeal from the raw material.

Chapter 7

Persistence

P resence allows us to leverage one of the most powerful, but underestimated, qualities of leadership—persistence. Persistence harnesses will, drive, commitment, and endurance— informed by presence—into one unconquerable force. If you are not present, you cannot be persistent. If you are not persistent, you will often stop just short of success.

This invaluable lesson came to me over several years of observing Artemis at work. Over the eight years that she has been with me, she has assumed the lead within every single herd in which she has resided, and there have been several. How? Persistence. A recent event demonstrated this perfectly. It happened when one of our horses, Brio, first arrived to live with us.

An enormous red-brown Lusitano (Portuguese bull-fighting horse), Brio stomped mightily off our trailer onto our driveway and surveyed his new home with large bright eyes. A long swath of mane draped over one side of his face almost to his flaring nostrils. With a loud and emphatic snort, he announced his arrival to our herd, who by now had all lined up excitedly along the north side of their paddock fence, six sets of ears pricked sharply forward.

Introducing a new horse to the herd is never an easy task. In most cases it's fraught with drama, screams, kicks, and bites as everyone negotiates the new terms. It can last anywhere from hours to months. And our gregarious and highly opinionated herd members usually have lots to discuss when there is change. Scott and I looked at each other and sighed in that "here we go again" kind of way. We led Brio to his holding pen—a separate but attached area where he could meet and get to know the others without clashing.

Brio had lived amongst stallions for much of his life. Seldom, if ever, did he encounter (up close anyway) mares. This is akin to a young man being raised motherless in a community of Hell's Angels. Lacking the usual discipline and cultural refinement that mares teach, Brio had not a single clue how to behave with mares or with a multigendered herd. This became utterly apparent when a week later we released Brio into the paddock with the others for his debut.

Like Godzilla he took over the city. Not once did he pause to check to see the established order or learn who belonged where. Naturally peaceful and conflict-averse, the horses complied, but they were not loyal to this new insurgent. Though Brio crowned himself king, he spent his days alone in one corner of the paddock while the others huddled together in the other. And where was Artemis in all this? She did not fight him. She simply, quietly, yet deliberately gave way. Artemis had another strategy.

I learned so much about power in those weeks. I learned how misuse of power creates compliance, but does not create respect or loyalty. I learned that horses generally will not resort to violence even when abused, and that even in nature, abuses of power can happen. When it does, it costs everyone including the abuser. But the most masterful teaching about power came from Artemis.

As lead mare, her role required her to sustain safety, connection, peace, freedom, and joy through her care and her presence. She was not wired to suddenly depart from her intrinsic nature as a leader and duke it out with the usurper. What an interesting conundrum Brio presented for Artemis. How to maintain those qualities in the face of a coup? Would she take up arms with the gnashing of teeth and hurling of hooves? But that would be counter to her leadership fidelity. And besides, Brio had easily another 700 pounds on her.

At first it appeared as if Artemis did nothing. I feared she had resigned herself to the new status quo and that the herd would be sad and depressed forever. But I had underestimated her. In fact she was leveraging one of the most potent elements of physics—time.

And time allowed Artemis one of the most overlooked, but powerful strategies of enlightened leadership—persistence. While most of us in modern life have grown to rely on speed and efficiency to get things done, we do so at significant cost. What would we do with a Brio in our midst? Many of us would acquiesce, some of us would complain, others would plot his arrest, but few would stand in such emboldened dignity as Artemis.

True to the conservation of energy that true leadership and living requires, Artemis saw no need for running around burning calories to take control of things. She let time do the work and used her presence to change the power dynamic. Yep, just like the old proverbial water on a stone. We are talking glacial. The field of safety, connection, and peace that she projected gently bent the others toward her leadership.

What evolved over the weeks that became months was a subtle yet clear shift of power. It was more like a ripening than a dramatic reclamation, more a gentle unfurling than a grand sweep. And then one morning when I went out to feed, I saw Brio quickly move away from Artemis in reaction to the faintest curl of her lip in his direction. I smiled to myself. She was back, and with her the equilibrium of the entire herd. Her persistence wore him out. Little by little her tiny requests, her subtle refusals, and the inertia of the other horses' positive responses to her nuanced leadership style won over his might.

CULTURALLY WE MISS TURNING TO THE LEADERSHIP SKILLS OF THOSE WHO HAVE QUIETER, YET POTENT, QUALITIES—THE KIND, THE THOUGHTFUL, THE QUIET, THE MINDFUL, THE EMPATHETIC.

What became of dear Brio? Well, true leadership serves the whole and that includes Brio. He learned a lot from the expert mentoring and modeling of Artemis. He found his right use of power, and with that he became friends with the others. He even landed his own unique role in the herd as the protector of the underdogs—in this case, our donkey, Kassie, and our partly blind mare, Blue. Even there Brio learned the finer distinctions of protection, merely standing quietly alongside Kassie or Blue at the hay box, ensuring they could eat uninterrupted by the others.

Persistence, born of and held by presence inside the long arc of time, is the superpower of wisdom-inspired leadership—in families, organizations, and relationships. In the movies, we don't see a lot of persistence demonstrated. It would be boring. Shifts in power dynamics are shown in dramatic fell-swoops of slick one-liners, a quick bullet, or bloody battle scene. We are conditioned to believe that power is akin to drama and grandiosity and think that the powerful make things happen instantly.

Culturally we miss turning to the leadership skills of those who have quieter, yet potent, qualities—the kind, the thoughtful, the quiet, the mindful, the empathetic. How might our institutions shift if we led with those virtues? What we can learn from Artemis is that leadership is incredibly refined, understated, and subtle.

The ability to stand up, step forward, stay motivated, and not give up in the face of certain failure is what makes the difference between good enough and exceptional. Look back at history to those committed to the art of persistence and you'll see their enormous contributions in their wake.

Abraham Lincoln failed in business at the age of 21. He was defeated in a legislative race at 22, he failed again at business at 24, had a nervous breakdown at 27, lost congressional races at 34 and 36, lost a senatorial race at 45, failed to become vice president at 47, and lost a senatorial race at 49. Yet he was elected president of the United States of America at age 52. The Dalai Lama, Mother Teresa, Harriet Tubman, and Nelson Mandela all persisted across long stretches of time to do their good work. Where would the world be without their persistence?

These times call for persistence in the face of failure. And the changes we see may at first look miniscule. Small micro-actions and mico-practices done over a stretch of time lead to immense changes. Don't let the seemingly slow appearance of change, either by impact or pace, undermine your ability to persevere.

SPIRAL POINT

JOURNAL QUESTIONS

- How does the story of Artemis reclaiming her power impact your sense of power, leadership, and change?

- What gets in the way of you being persistent? Is there anything in your life now that needs your persistence? What is it?

EXERCISES

- Write a letter to yourself from five years in the future—your most optimally desired future. Describe your future life in clear detail to your present self. What has changed? What did you do to get there? What advice does your future self have for you? With what do you need to persevere?

- Make a vision board of your most desired life five years in the future. Tear out magazine images, words, poetry, whatever, and glue it onto a 8½" x 11" piece of cardboard (or larger). Put it somewhere that you will see it often, and set an intention to persistently go for the life you want to create.

PART IV
Safety

All creatures must learn that there exist predators.
Without this knowing, a person will be unable to
negotiate safely within their own forest without being
devoured. To understand the predator is to become a
mature animal who is not vulnerable out of
naïveté, inexperience, or foolishness.

CLARISSA PINKOLA ESTÉS,
Women Who Run With the Wolves:
Myths and Stories of the Wild Woman Archetype[1]

W ithout safety—emotional, physical, mental, and spiritual— we are merely prey animals, easily devoured by a world that seeks to change or manipulate us. We cannot lead a flying change without the foundation of safety to stabilize our efforts.

Creating safety inside our relationships, our families, and our organizations liberates enormous possibilities. Without safety there is disconnect, fear, and erosion of trust. This requires us to be savvy about our environment, internal and external, and the predators that exist there. Some predators take human form and some take the form of beliefs that eat at us, habits that wolf down our creativity, or cultural norms that corner us. Identifying predatory behaviors and habits in ourselves and others (and toward ourselves and others) is one step toward well-being. Another step is in creating social systems and structures that support safety.

In the horse herd, there are structures in place for protection, ensuring the safety of every member. But these structures also support a reciprocity of safety within the herd, holding each member accountable for the safety of everyone else. Space between herd members is a conduit not only for safety, but connection and communication as well. Clearly defined roles and responsibilities through each horse's rightful place support authentic communication and a robust resilience against predators. And finally, the literal position of leadership—which is not on top, or out front, but behind—ensures the ongoing legacy of its welfare.

In this section you will learn to create safety for yourself and others through these three essential principles so that you and others around you can thrive.

Chapter 8

Space

O f all the lessons the horses have taught me, the concept of space is perhaps the most fascinating. Space—this vast, invisible element we cannot see—plays an essential role in supporting every single thing that we do. While it's tempting to take it for granted, understanding space—our own personal space, the space of others, the spaces we find ourselves in externally— and learning how to navigate and create agency within it, gives us protective dominion over our lives. It also helps create safety for others.

Peripersonal neurons are cells in the brain that monitor the space around the body. "Their activity rises like a Geiger counter to indicate the location of objects entering a margin of safety," writes author and professor of neuroscience and psychology at Princeton University Michael S. A. Graziano. "In the psychology literature of the 1960s, *personal space* referred to a social safety buffer around the body. In the past few years, researchers have begun to realize just how deep the connection runs between the personal space of psychology and the peripersonal neurons on the brain."[1]

Graziano calls our invisible protective bubble the *second skin* that is constantly switched on like a force field. We all have one. Some keep their bubble close like a wetsuit, others project it like a circus tent. And sometimes a person's bubble can vary in size depending upon the circumstance.[2]

Obviously, being able to negotiate tight spaces, weave in and out of obstacles, and avoid sharp corners as we walk through a room are all important abilities that we achieve thanks to our peripersonal neurons. The part of personal space that is far more refined yet still governed by the same neurons has to do with emotional, mental, psychic, and spiritual space. It too expands and contracts depending upon the person and the circumstances.

Space bubbles are dynamic; they shape-shift depending upon the environment and the person. In early research, personal space was thought to be the area within which others were invited, "almost like a sitting room, something arranged for the purpose of accepting in friends and organizing conversation," writes Graziano. But later studies revealed that the space bubble is a protective agent, and defines the boundary line you don't want other people to cross.[3]

WE'VE BEEN SOCIALIZED AWAY FROM OUR INSTINCTIVE SENSE OF TAKING UP SPACE EMOTIONALLY, PSYCHICALLY, AND SPIRITUALLY.

Several experiments have yielded fascinating findings about the dynamics of personal space. One consistent revelation is that personal space expands with anxiety or stress. The more anxious you are, the larger your bubble with regard to other people. I would add the more sensitive you are, the larger your bubble too. However, when you feel confident or at ease, your bubble shrinks.

One study looked at the spaces surrounding powerful leaders. For example, presidents are notorious for having thirty-foot bubbles around them. President Kennedy, surrounded by fans and admirers, would walk into a room and seemingly part the crowds with his space bubble. Closer research reveals that individuals like Kennedy might possess small personal space fields, but everyone around them creates a nervous respectful distance of about thirty feet with their space bubbles. In large spaces, most peoples' bubbles are plump and roundish. Yet when people are crowded together, such as at a rock concert, the balloon compresses, and tends to stick out farther in the front than the sides or behind.[4]

PERSONAL SPACE

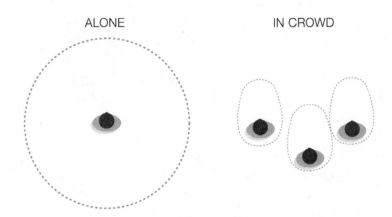

ALONE   IN CROWD

Animals also have a small portable territory that is often referred to as a flight zone. If, when you were a kid, you ever tried to catch a lizard or a frog, you learned that there was an invisible line between your ability to be near the creature in an effort to seize them and suddenly sending them scurrying away. As a young girl trying to catch my horse on my stepfather's 3,000-acre ranch, I discovered much to my dismay that my horse's space bubble was easily 600 feet. Before I even saw him, he was fleeing into the next pasture. Some days I just fell down in teary frustration after hours of trying to bribe him, coerce him, and lure him to my halter—all to no avail. From this pitiless education I learned how to engage with his space bubble in a way that made me intriguing to him so I could catch him. It meant that I had to take up space too, so that our bubbles could participate with one another.

Our space bubbles can be compromised or altered in different ways. *Dyspraxia*, for example, is a rare but life-altering condition in which a person fails to sense their own personal space. Domestication actually shrinks the space bubbles of animals—the more domesticated the animal, the smaller their personal space.[5]

In the years of working with people, I've noticed a kind of social dyspraxia. It's as if—like domesticated farm animals—we've been

socialized away from our instinctive sense of taking up space emotionally, psychically, and spiritually. We have no idea how to sense,
create, enforce, and navigate this kind of space. The result is that
we are constantly pretzeling ourselves to fit in. Often our work at
EQUUS involves rewilding people back to their felt sense of all
aspects of their space.

Pam and her husband Leon were a highly . . . let's say domesticated couple. They came to EQUUS all the way from Alaska, hoping
to gain clarity on their next steps together. Raised inside strict evan-
gelical Christian households, their sense of themselves was largely
defined by harsh dogma. But in recent years, both of these bright
people began to sense there was something more out there to life,
and they felt a strong pull toward self-discovery. They noticed that
the church condemned things that brought them joy or evoked
openness, so they decided to choose joy, and in doing so were forced
to split from their community and their families. And this left them
feeling vulnerable, alone, and afraid.

People breaking free of dogma—religious, corporate, or otherwise—
and searching for trustworthy answers often feel conflicted about turning to other humans, since all we offer is just one more opinion. At
this formative stage of someone's selfhood, they have no interest in
trading one ideology for another. Horses are ideal companions inside
this crucial exploration.

On their first day with us, Pam and Leon wandered the arena to
greet our herd. This first encounter is essential to witness exactly
how people are showing up (in the raw, so to speak) without any
instruction or adjustment to how they are being. The horses always
reflect what needs to be seen, and it's always different for every
single person. Normally respectful, our horses behaved oddly impo-
lite toward Pam and Leon. Some of them rubbed all over them,
others brushed past them rudely. Pam and Leon giggled nervously.

"What's that like?" I asked after a while. Cisco was still using Leon
as a scratching post.

"I think he likes me," responded Leon. Pam beamed. "Yeah," she said.

"And what does it actually *feel* like?" I pressed. Cisco continued.
Leon furrowed his brow. Pam looked down.

"Well, not so nice actually," responded Leon finally as Cisco pressed so hard on his back while moving his head up and down that Leon had to catch himself from tipping over. "I feel like I don't really matter. And he's awfully big and it doesn't feel nice to be nearly shoved over." Leon may have been speaking about his church or his family and friends or any other influence that had convinced him that he had to live small.

We spent the morning unpacking what it felt like in their bodies when something entered their space in a disrespectful manner. I asked them to pay attention to subtle shifts in their bodies—a tightening in the chest, a gnawing in their bellies—when they considered various religious concepts, people, or events that they claimed seemed just normal to their life. We explored what taking up space meant for Leon and Pam— in their case, defining what did and did not belong inside their emotional, psychic, and spiritual bubbles. Until that day, neither of them felt that they had the right to this fundamental aspect of being alive. This is the impact of growing up inside circumstances such as brutally strict households, fundamentalist religions, and other chronically traumatic scenarios. It creates domesticated adults who are numb to their bodies' personal navigation and alarm system, loyal to an ideology or group over their own self-wisdom.

Thanks to our peripersonal neurons, our bodies are perfect transmitters that tell us loud and clear all kinds of important information—like when we are somewhere we don't belong, or something is not right for us, or when we've split from our personal truth to honor someone else's. Our gut feelings signal to us what is safe, life sustaining, or threatening—even if our rational mind cannot explain it. We say *he felt creepy* or *that made me sick* or *my heart sank*—all common expressions of how our limbic system translates into strong emotional feedback.

"Agency is the technical term for the feeling of being in charge of your life: knowing where you stand, knowing that you have a say in what happens to you, knowing that you have some ability to change your circumstances," writes professor of psychiatry at Boston University School of Medicine Bessel van der Kolk. "Agency starts with what scientists call interoception, our awareness of our subtle sensory, body-based feelings: the greater that awareness, the greater our potential to control our lives. This *noticing of sensations* is the very neurobiology of our own selfhood.[6]

We have found in our work, however, that most people ignore their bodies' signals. They learn to hide from themselves, preferring to reside in the region above the neck. "Sometimes we use our minds not to discover facts, but to hide them," writes neuroscientist Antonio Damasio, pointing out the deep divide between our sense of self and the sensory life of our bodies.[7]

Pam was looking increasingly distressed as she began to spend more time in her body. It can be, at first, overwhelming to return to it. I asked her how she was doing.

"We were told as children that our bodies were the source of sin," Pam said, looking down. "I don't even know the first thing about relating to it."

Shame, trauma, and oppressive ideologies create a population unequipped to deal with the body's sensations. "But I discipline my body and keep it under control," commands the Bible.[8] The price for squelching, controlling, ignoring, or distorting the body's messages is being unable to detect what is truly dangerous or harmful for you and, just as bad, what is safe and nourishing, emphasizes van der Kolk. "Self-regulation depends on having a friendly relationship with your body. Without it you have to rely on external regulation—from medication, alcohol, constant reassurance, or compulsive compliance with the wishes of others."[9]

Pam and Leon spent the day feeling their sensations. Then they diagramed their individual space bubbles on ground with lengths of rope. Pam's was circular and about twelve feet around her. Leon's was more like a triangle and a bit smaller. I asked them to step inside their roped territory.

"How does that feel, to have that space?" I asked. They both smiled broadly. Pam exhaled.

"I can breathe; I can feel myself," said Pam. "And it feels good!"

"That good feeling is your body telling you that it is right, that you are in alignment with yourself," I said. "That's how you know what's really true. Now you don't have to believe someone else's truth."

Now Pam and Leon were not only sensing their right to their own personal space, but also a natural understanding of their boundaries, i.e., what they should and should not accept within their personhood so that they may stay aligned with the life they wanted to create. They explored their bodily posture inside their bubbles and noticed themselves standing taller, with their feet wider apart, their chests more lifted. "I feel bigger," noticed Pam.

Social psychologist Amy Cuddy asserts that our posture not only shapes others' perceptions of us, but our perceptions of ourselves. Some findings reveal that it even changes our body chemistry.[10] In observing clients learning to take up their space and claim their boundaries, I have found that the entire unfolding exists in concert as a powerful and positive gestalt—posture, confidence, space, selfhood, agency, perception. So, yes, I agree that chemistry changes. And not just with the space bearer, but the others around them.

As soon as the couple had created their bubbles and claimed their agency, an interesting shift occurred within the herd. Instead of being bored or dismissive of Pam and Leon, the horses became instantly respectful and curious. They stood around the pair in a semicircle at a courteous yet connected distance, their ears pricked forward. Then Cisco stepped forward. Horses often test the new normal to make sure it's for real. He marched toward Leon's triangle, aiming for a good head scratch again. Intuitively, Leon put his hand in the air—his body erect and strong this time, his feet wide apart. "No," Leon commanded. Cisco stopped abruptly. Cisco's ears pricked forward in attentiveness. Then he lowered his head and let out a huge yawn—a positive emotional processing response to external stimulus.

"Wow! I thought he'd be mad," said Leon. "I thought he'd feel rejected."

In coaching and therapy, we call this moment a *disconfirming experience*—a breakthrough learning opportunity when a longstanding belief is challenged by a presenting reality. In fact, Cisco felt incredibly safe now that Leon knew how to protect his own space. To Cisco, Leon was now more trustworthy because he understood the physics and dynamics of space—his and, by association, others'—which creates safety for all. From Cisco's point of view, he'd much rather have a companion he could trust than a scratching post. Horses wonderfully reflect how space and healthy boundaries feel good and are beneficial for everyone concerned. The positive reinforcement is essential to learning about space, because humans—who are domesticated away from these essential skills—often deliver conflicting and sometimes even hostile feedback to those creating space and boundaries. We'll look into this more in the upcoming chapter on rewilding when we examine tribal shaming.

Space allows us the freedom to move without physically (as well as emotionally and psychically) bumping into each other. In herd dynamics it safeguards against bumping into one another, ensuring efficient response to danger. When we apply this principle to organizational structures, couples, and families, the safety and well-being of the system improves.

The herd reveals that space does not separate; it connects. It is a dynamic and fluid conduit of invisible and essential pieces of information that need not be limited by proximity. When Uncle Bob and I were miles apart (and sometimes continents and oceans away), his messages would come to me via signs and signals. If I truly listened (I confess, oftentimes regretfully I did not), I'd pick up the phone and call him. "So you heard me calling out to you, did you?" he'd reply with a chuckle.

With beloveds, friends, and family, we may experience this connection across distance, having a sense of someone we love who is far away. When we reach out, we learn they were needing us. "And we are put on earth a little space, that we might learn to bear the beams of love," writes William Blake.[11] If we all filled out space with more confidence and permission, knowing its potential to connect, just think of the possibilities.

SPIRAL POINT

JOURNAL QUESTIONS

- Do you honor your space? Do you honor the space of others? How do you navigate space?

- If you gave yourself permission, how much more space would you take up? What would that look like in daily life?

EXERCISES

- Take a piece of paper and draw a circle in the middle of it. In the middle of the circle write your name. Think about all the people, activities, and projects that bring you joy or feel life giving. Place them inside your circle. Now think of all the people, activities, and projects that diminish you or your energy and place them outside your circle. Look at the diagram you've created. What does it tell you?

- For this exercise, you will need a piece of string or rope about thirty feet long. Stand in a spacious room or out-doors somewhere and close your eyes and feel where your authentic space bubble is. What shape is it? How big is it? Now take the rope or string and make that shape around you. Make sure it feels large enough and is just the right shape. Stand in the middle of the space bubble you have created. How does it feel to take up space? How does it feel to claim your space?

Chapter 9

Place

One of the benefits of taking up our own personal space is that we become more acquainted with ourselves. *Who am I? What are my gifts and strengths? What are my values?* These are questions that begin to emerge inside the psychic space that is allowed to have its dominion. We are no longer satisfied with being identified by what we do ("VP of Sales") or our relationships ("Karen's wife") or our attributes ("I'm an introvert"). We sense there is a more significant dignity to claim. I call this finding our place. In contrast to location, place in this context refers to an existential place—a sense of meaningful purpose.

When I first introduce a client to our herd, we hang out on the other side of the arena fence and observe. I point out that each member has a role, and with that role a set of responsibilities—their place in the herd. A herd member's place is determined by their character and intrinsic aptitudes. Artemis, the alpha mare, is standing quietly, maintaining the grounding quiet presence for everyone. Brio, the protector, who takes things very seriously, is stalwartly standing watch over Blue. Cisco, Dante, and Cimarron are whirling about in mock sparring, running, playing, and bucking about. They are the herd's comedic relief. And Kassie the donkey protects from predators.

Over the years of observing each of our horses, I've come to see that when they are given space, they begin to assume their rightful place. They not only have their roles within their herd but also within the EQUUS work. Cisco, for example, tends to resonate and work with young men who are seeking permission to say no to negative influences. Artemis evokes and tutors the servant leader. Blue gives permission for vulnerability and empathy and will also march right up to someone who—we come to discover later—has grappled with blindness in some way. Cimarron is the trickster. He creates amazing learning conditions through artful play and provocation.

To find our existential place, it is helpful to differentiate between the *how* and the *why* of our life. When theologian, author, and psychiatrist Gerald May refers to the *how*, he means our efficiencies in life—the practicalities of daily living in our functional roles and activities.

In contrast, May says that the *why* is our fundamental spirit, "the wellspring of our vitality, what we want to be efficient *for*."[1] It is the purposeful underpinning of meaning in our life. For some it is love, for others it is creativity, and others it is social change. You will find your why if you reflect upon the continuing thread of significance that runs through your lifetime. "I create conditions for others to thrive," declared Leon when he found his why. Parenting his children, running his import business, and volunteering for the Boys Club of America are how he serves his why.

> WHENEVER I SEE A LIFESTYLE THAT IS HINGED ON SPEED, EFFICIENCY, AND HECTIC BUSYNESS, I SEE A LIFE RUN BY SHAME.

We can get so caught up in the efficiencies of our life that we lose sight of our why, and hence our place. Our why should always be our first fidelity. Our efficiencies serve our why. But it can get mixed up. When I was a young parent, I liked to do fun things with my children (my *how*) because I loved them (my *why*), but often I became preoccupied with efficiency. One day, I wanted to take my children to the playground, but my son wanted to read at home and my daughter was engrossed in a game. I started to become frustrated. "No! We're going to the playground!" I ordered. The kids got into the car begrudgingly and we had a terrible morning. In being hyperfocused on the how (my plans), I lost sight of the why (love). If I'd remembered my fidelity to love, I would have reworked the morning to just be with the kids in their own way so that love was truly served.

The Why and the How

The why of our life is the thread of meta-purpose and meaning that runs throughout our lives—*to love*, for example, or *to see the gifts of others*. The how of our life refers to the service, efficiencies, and actions we engage to serve our why—e.g., *taking my children to school* or *meeting with my team*.

When efficiencies are out of balance, it is a symptom of something else—shame. In my case with the kids, I was run by a sense of not being a good enough parent. Whenever I see a lifestyle that is hinged on speed, efficiency, and hectic busyness, I see a life run by shame. We think we can outrun it and so we skip like a stone across the water, straining to get to the other shore without descending into shame's depths.

Shame is our ongoing and corrosive belief that we are inherently broken, flawed, or bad, therefore unworthy of belonging, love, or connection. Sometimes shame is a feeling, often it is more like a state or a habit of belief patterns. Our shame-states and belief patterns are so close to us that we don't notice them. It just feels normal. We all carry shame to some degree because our collective systems (family, school, church) use shame to keep us within their fold.

If we do not become aware of it, shame prevents us from taking our place. Life feels meaningless, purposeless, and relentless. We live our life anxiously skimming across the surface, yearning for something else. That period of my life before Uncle Bob took me to see the wild horses for the first time was a time when shame had got the better of me. Crushed by the loss of a child and the end of a yet another marriage, I was skating across the surface of my life, racing to get to some other side so I didn't have to feel the disgrace of it all. Part of the reason shame grabbed me so hard during that time was my silence around my circumstances.

"Shame derives its power from being unspeakable. If we cultivate enough awareness about shame to name it and speak to it, we've basically cut it off at the knees," writes Brené Brown, author and research professor at the University of Houston Graduate College of Social Work. "Shame hates having words wrapped around it. If we speak shame, it begins to wither."[2] Shame denies us place. The most pervasive and underexamined shame is the belief that we are separate from love, God, the universe, life force. It's so pervasive, in fact, that we don't even call it shame.

Brown further asserts that shame "lurks in familiar places" and she has defined twelve "shame categories" based on a career of social science research:[3]

- Appearance and body image
- Money and work
- Motherhood/fatherhood
- Family
- Parenting
- Mental and physical health
- Addiction
- Sex
- Ageing
- Religion
- Being stereotyped or labeled
- Trauma

Several years ago we had the opportunity to work with a consortium of Native people from all around the Four Corners region of Utah, Colorado, Arizona, and New Mexico. This group of about twenty-five participants represented various social activists, healthcare practitioners, and community leaders. Given the many versions of the "The Promise" story I had heard over the years that had originated from the original peoples of the Four Corners area, I was excited to witness this group engaging with the horses. I confess that I projected all kinds of reunion scenarios and envisioned that the day would be filled with joy and laughter. Instead, something entirely different happened.

When they all entered the arena to meet the horses, the horses responded in a bizarre fashion. Normally when people enter the herd, our horses are curious, or they may show off, be agitated, or take turns meeting each person, or, in some instances, lie down in an expression of tremendous trust. In this case, the horses responded with downright boredom. They kept perusing the fence line, looking for blades of dead, brown grass. They meandered aimlessly and sauntered past each person like they were invisible. Some even pressed on the gate, wanting to leave. Not one horse acknowledged any person in that entire group. It was as if the people weren't there.

I had never seen this response from our horses before. I was completely baffled. Why were the participants so uninteresting to the horses? This was curious to me, especially given the nature of the group—a collection of caring and committed people who dedicate their lives to advocating for the earth and for their communities.

One thing I've learned over decades of working with people and horses is that I'm not the one with the answers. That role typically belongs among the horses or, ultimately, the participants. We are taught as coaches and facilitators to have a beginner's mind, to ask powerful questions, and to take on the mindset that the client knows better than we do about what is right for them. I concede that while this is an honorable mindset to which I always aspire, there is some part of me somewhere that has at least a hunch about what might be happening. In this case, I was genuinely clueless. So when we began some dialogue about what the horses were doing, my questions were downright earnest, perhaps even slightly frantic. I felt out of my depth. "What were the horses reflecting?" I asked the participants. "If we assume that the horses have a gift of teaching, what might that be?"

It was a difficult morning for all of us and the situation required a gentle, open hand to facilitate their revelations. As the horses were illuminating, the fact was indeed that the group *wasn't there*. Even though their bodies were in the arena, their presence was not. Through questions and dialogue, we discovered together that every member of the group held shame for simply being alive, brought about by their collective historical trauma as displaced indigenous people.

"You took us from our land, our spirituality, and our families," said Uncle Bob, describing how white Australians systematically wiped out his people—a story shared by indigenous peoples around the world. "We are like the walking dead. How are we supposed to survive if we do not know our place?" Aboriginal Australians were hunted, trapped, displaced, and owned. The story of exile, abduction of women and children, genocide, and land dispossession is as old as humanity, yet it still lives inside the very tissues of those whose relatives experienced it firsthand.

For the Native peoples of the United States, the blood remains in the soil. In 1830, the federal Indian Removal Act called for the displacement of the Cherokee, Chickasaw, Choctaw, Creek, and Seminole, forcing nearly 100,000 Natives out of their homeland. The dangerous journey from the southern states to the newly formed Indian Territory in what is now Oklahoma is referred to as the Trail of Tears. Over 4,000 Cherokee people died of cold, hunger, and disease. In 1850, California passed the Act for the Government and Protection of Indians facilitating the ongoing destruction of their culture and land. It also legalized slavery and legitimized the buying and selling of Native children.[4] Like the Stolen Generations of Aboriginal Australians, Native American children were also stolen from their parents and raised in institutions. When an entire people are displaced, they are exiled not only from a physical locale, but from their souls. It guts them and their reason for existing for generations.

Clinical neuropsychologist Mario Martinez lectures worldwide on the ways in which cultural beliefs affect health and success. He asserts that there are three archetypal wounds inflicted upon us by cultural settings: shame, betrayal, and abandonment. Each archetypal wound has an antidote. For betrayal, it is loyalty; for abandonment, it is commitment; and for shame, honor.[5] To tend to the group's collective shame, we asked the individuals to reflect on any time in their life in which they experienced honor—perhaps a time when they protected someone from bullying, or when they met a challenge with integrity. We then invited them to feel that memory in their body. Igniting those positive somatic experiences created a sudden shift. Then, after several moments, the entire group settled into a felt sense of their right to simply be there. It was an internal and seemingly imperceptible change—nothing I could have tracked. But the horses did.

As if awakened from a spell, the horses snapped to bright, interested attention. Ears pricked forward with acute curiosity; they began happily mingling with the group, exploring each person with their large, soft noses, one by one. Then they contentedly settled amidst the people, creating another larger herd comprised now of four-leggeds and two-leggeds. The horses' yawns, exhales, and blows—all indications of positive emotional release—signified that the new constellation of connection was much more beneficial to them than their previous state of boredom.

This scenario revealed to all of us that the simple taking of our rightful place within the horse herd created more positive energy for all. While it was obvious that the people benefited from their connection to themselves and to the horses, the horses also benefitted from the people's reconnection with their place within all creation.

Even though this is an extreme example, it's been my experience that no one—regardless of race, class, or status—is immune to shame around one's sense of place. Even some people who belong to the most privileged 1 percent can carry a shame that erodes their sense of the right to exist. In response, they either overperform, mask themselves, or try to disappear. It's subtle but real, and the horses reflect it with heartbreaking accuracy.

When we don't take our place—or when we take our place with ambivalence—we deny the world our gifts. Claiming our existential place, informed by our why, is our birthright. It is also essential to creating a flying lead change. We cannot leap into the unknown without the grounded origins of our right footing.

SPIRAL POINT

JOURNAL QUESTIONS

- Notice if some kind of shame lurks underneath all of your busyness and the endless to-do lists that keep you running fast on the wheel of efficiency, rather than living a life of meaning. Trace it back to your earliest memories and see what core shame story you told yourself about you when you were a small child because of how someone treated you. Perhaps the story goes something like *I am not enough* or *I am alone.* Confront it, see its falseness, and write yourself a new story statement, e.g., *I am a powerful, loving person who is surrounded by support.*

- What is the why of your life, i.e., the reason you took birth to manifest your own unique calling or purpose in the world? Journal about it. What are all the ways you want to manifest your why in your life?

EXERCISES

- Notice when you are triggered by one of the three archetypal wounds: shame, betrayal, or abandonment. When that happens, pause and summon its antidote (honor, loyalty, or commitment consecutively). Recall a time when you felt one of those three depending on your trigger. Now feel that memory in your body and continue to experience it viscerally for two minutes. This is how we begin to heal from such wounds.

- On a piece of cardboard, make a collage of your why life—your purpose, your existential place. Do not use words, only images. Keep it somewhere that you can see it every day.

Chapter 10

Leading from Behind

When we find our place, a natural process occurs that provokes us to assist others to find and serve theirs. We place ourselves in service to humanity, calling forth the greatness in others. To me, this is the highest definition of leadership—be it within a family, an organization, a project, or one's own self-actualization. Our positional orientation as leaders defines our ability to successfully evoke capacity in others. What is that orientation? From behind, not out in front.

A delightful story from the Victorian era comes to mind. Lady Jennie Jerome was the American mother of Winston Churchill. Admired for her beauty and dignity, she glided through the loftiest social circles in Great Britain. On consecutive nights, Ms. Jerome dined with two of England's premier politicians—Benjamin Disraeli and William Gladstone—rivals who were competing for the position of prime minister. When questioned about her impressions of the men, it's rumored that Ms. Jerome said, "When I left the dining room after sitting next to Gladstone, I thought he was the cleverest man in England. But when I sat next to Disraeli I thought I was the cleverest woman."[1]

Perhaps you know leaders like Gladstone—confident individuals who exude wit, intelligence, and prowess. You cannot help but notice them because they make every effort to parade their brilliance. However, I'll wager that you'd prefer to follow someone like Disraeli—a leader who would rather draw out the best in you than strut their personal greatness.

When, as a leader, you take yourself off center stage and place others there to shine instead, you are practicing the masterful art of leading from behind. It is a skill that not only creates new leaders within the system, but ensures the safety of the collective by bringing out the power in others.

To find the lead horse in a herd, you wouldn't look for the one out front. You would look for the one at the back. Horses lead from behind. This is demonstrated most obviously (but not solely) in how they physically move the herd. The lead horse positions himself or herself behind the ones in their charge and literally pushes them ahead. This encourages the horses being led to actually be out in the fore. The softest of requests, a mere thought or shift of energy can move an entire band of twenty. Or sometimes the guidance is delivered more firmly—with a hard eye, a flattening of ears, or a toss of the head.

Being urged to the front lines of the herd by the leader develops confidence and courage in the others. They then become the eyes of the herd, the first to encounter danger and new experiences. In this way, nature designs leadership to be cultivated throughout the herd in preparation for succession, encouraging less confident horses to move out front, thus becoming more self-assured so that when the lead horse passes on or retires, the next leader has been mentored for years to be confident. This way of leading empowers the confidence and greatness of others and creates a super-structure, ensuring not only the immediate safety of the herd, but an entire legacy of leadership.

Toshio was the newly appointed CEO of a health-care company based in Japan. His board of directors sent him and his leadership team to EQUUS so that they could all become better acquainted and build cohesion among them. After spending the morning working with connection, we spent the rest of the afternoon exploring leadership in action as informed by the connection cultivated in the hours prior. If you connect with your team, colleague, or family member before you take action, the results are far more successful. We emphasize *connection before action* and *relationship before task* to our clients.

We haltered up several horses and paired each horse with a person. We instructed the team to lead their horses not by being out in front of them pulling, but by positioning themselves alongside their horses, at their shoulders. The position of the human in this exercise is important. If they position themselves at the rear of the horse, to drive the horse forward, this would be the most dominant. If they positioned themselves at the front, the horse becomes the most dominant (able to push the human forward). But shoulder-to-shoulder (the most friendly position) encourages the horse to be slightly out front by a nose, building their confidence while the human leader has optimal influence on the horse at his or her side. After a few minutes of demonstrating this version of leading from behind, we handed the lead ropes to each team member, including Toshio.

The others struggled alongside their horses with various levels of success. But Toshio had a completely different modus operandi. Without hesitation (and hence without getting present and connected), he grabbed the lead rope from my hand, slung it over his shoulder for leverage, and literally dragged the horse behind him like a donkey around the arena. After a few moments, even the others stopped to watch the spectacle. I deliberately did not rush in to correct him, and instead allowed the whole scenario to play out for a while and do its own teaching, as only equine-assisted learning can do.

"Is his horse really lazy?" asked an onlooker, nodding toward the sleek, muscular, tall, and leggy thoroughbred doggedly tromping behind Toshio.

"Looking at the horse's physique, would you say he is?" I countered. It's always best to point people toward their own ability to see through a situation into what's actually happening.

"Nope," she smiled.

"Toshio's leadership style might lead one to think that, however," I offered.

After a while, Toshio suddenly realized the eyes of the whole group were on him. He stopped, a little embarrassed, but to his credit, he was instantly curious. Everyone began to chuckle lightheartedly.

"What?" he asked, a little defensively.

I asked the others to lead their horses in the way that they were learning so that Toshio could observe. As the moments passed, each participant grew increasingly skilled at guiding their horses slightly ahead of them, and as they did the horses became more bright and engaged. Eventually the horse-human pairs became so synchronized in movement it was hard to tell who was leading whom. Toshio watched for some time.

"Please ask everyone to come back," he requested. The team gathered back into the center of the arena.

"I have something to share with each of you," he said, not hiding his emotion. "What I was doing out there with my horse . . . that is how I have always led. I went completely on autopilot. In spite of instruction, in spite of all the preparation to be present and connected, I did what I always do," he paused and gathered himself. "I just pulled myself out front, ignored the horse, and trudged on."

The team was profoundly impacted by this show of vulnerability and accountability. You could actually feel the trust enter the space.

"My way of leading not only cost me . . . I . . . I was exhausted out there. And lonely. It also cost my horse. He felt like a lead weight behind me. I don't want to lead you like this," Toshio continued. "I want to do it this new way. I need your help to remind me."

It's moments like these that give me hope for humanity. If the horses can instruct a high-performing leader—one who wields enormous influence in hundreds of thousands of lives—in the right use of power, then real change is possible. That's what I would call a flying lead change moment.

Uncle Bob also led from behind. When we first met, I wanted to defer to his wisdom and decisions, especially around my presentation of his work. I would ask him what to do, or how to do it, or when, or even if. We easily hand our power over to authority figures, whether it be a church, a CEO, a spiritual teacher, the news, or a doctor, to do the thinking for us. In response to my deferment, Uncle Bob would always say a very succinct, "Well, what do *you* think?" or "What do *you* feel?" and leave it at that. A gentle nudge to the fore.

People in positions of power—from parent to priest to president—can and do create followers. In contrast to a highly successful multimillion-year-old system, creating followers is a dangerous game, making the herd vulnerable to predators in all manifestations.

Do you lead from behind, creating leaders? Or you do lead in the front, creating followers? This is a question worth asking ourselves in various contexts from organizational to familial. What does leading from behind look like in the human context?

Here's a list of attributes that I've collected by watching those who lead from behind (horse and human):

Curiosity. They are learners instead of knowers. Instead of having all the right answers, they are curious about what they can learn. They are also curious about the people around them. They ask helpful questions.

Listening. They spend less time talking and more time listening.

Confidence. You can only see what you are. If you are critical with yourself, you'll be critical of others. If you see your strengths and gifts, you'll see it in others. Leaders who lead from behind know their own gifts and strengths, which naturally allows them to see those attributes in others.

Humility. Like Toshio, they are open to being wrong, having more to learn, and respectful of others. Confidence and humility are not polarities—they are complementary.

Trust. These folks trust themselves and others (and therefore surround themselves with those they trust), and they trust something larger than themselves (the universe, the divine, grace, the infinite, God . . . whatever you want to call it).

They are not the most interesting person in the room. My friend and colleague, the leadership coach Rich Litvin, says, "If you are the most interesting person in the room, you are in the wrong room." Great leaders surround themselves with amazing people, and they create conditions for learning from and being inspired by those around them.

Kind, calm, and clear. They have a grounded firmness about them that is a blend of these three elements. I'm differentiating between niceness and kindness here, too. Kindness can tell hard truths, set boundaries, challenge, and make difficult decisions that clearly cut away what no longer belongs.

Their feet move the least. When observing a herd, you'll notice the leader is the one who moves the least, conserving energy for the important stuff. Leaders, parents, and professionals will often micromanage, rescue, or run alongside their team in an attempt to lead them properly. Good leaders provoke others to come up with solutions rather than offer solutions themselves.

Delight. Being positioned behind frees these people up to see the big picture in front of them and allows them to assess how everyone is contributing. This brings a natural state of appreciation for what is being accomplished. From here, shout-outs are easy. They celebrate the wins often.

Modeling. It's not what they say, it's how they *be*. They walk their talk.

Vulnerability. They are vulnerable and open to their humanity, as well as to the humanity of others. They see vulnerability as a strength. They courageously embrace failure.

Caring. They care personally for each person in their charge and for the system as a whole.

Present. They are attentive, mindful, and in the moment.

You have more power than you might realize. All it takes is just a little shift in position to see it. Head on back to the rear, and then liberate the human capital of others in front of you through your presence and care. When we create a safer environment through our masterful stewardship that emboldens confidence, there's nowhere we can't go together.

SPIRAL POINT

JOURNAL QUESTIONS

- Many people don't consider themselves leaders because they are not out front. Where do you lead from behind? Are there places in your life you are a leader, but you didn't know it because you were not out front? Describe them.

- Go through the list of leadership qualities above. Which ones do you want to cultivate? Which ones surprised you?

EXERCISES

- Practice leading from behind with those you care for. When they come to you with a problem or issue, rather than solving it or rescuing them, nudge them to the fore by asking powerful questions and supporting their empowerment.

- Is there someone in your life you are trying to drag along? Challenge yourself to reorient yourself to a different position with this person, and empower them to take their own steps forward.

PART V
Connection

We do not "come into" this world, we come *out* of it, as leaves from a tree. As the ocean "waves," the universe "peoples."

ALAN WATTS,
The Book: On the Taboo Against Knowing Who You Are[1]

We are hardwired for connection. Our bodies are literally designed to know, experience, and manifest connection in all its forms. Even more accurately, our bodies are a part of the intricate whole. But somewhere in our collective historic imperative, a misunderstanding occurred—an illusory perception of separation. From there entire cultures, structures, and belief systems perpetuated this one false idea: we are separate.

Loneliness, disconnection, and isolation are pervasive, especially in industrialized nations. A 2018 nationwide study from research firm Ipsos and health insurer Cigna found about half of adults surveyed either sometimes or always feel lonely or isolated. Among those between the ages of 18 to 22, 69 percent reported feelings of isolation, even when they were around others, and 68 percent said they feel like no one really knows them well.[2] More than just a negative experience, isolation and disconnect makes us sick, to the same degree as smoking, alcoholism, and obesity. A 2015 meta-review of 70 studies showed that loneliness increases the risk of your chance of prematurely dying by 26 percent.[3]

Our work together is to break this trance of disconnect and live into our birthright of belonging. As you'll see in the coming pages, this requires not just shifting our beliefs, but by practicing specific behaviors and actions that work to undo the lie of separation. According to the 56-million-year-old equine system, connection is the byproduct of four specific elements: belonging, requests, vulnerability, and engaging what I call the *Invisibles.* A flying lead change relies on all these elements of connection in order to be executed well.

Chapter 11

Belonging

I define belonging as an intrinsic, relational, unconditional acceptance within our circumstances. It's a sense of being entirely inside one's element. In contrast to fitting into a particular social circle, belonging is an unconditional state. Belonging is how a tree moves inside the soil, or a bird takes to the air.

Belonging is not so much an achievement as it is a birthright. But absent a culture that is informed by belonging, we are born into exile and shapeshift ourselves to belong to something or someone. A disconnected society seeks to return home in myriad dysfunctional ways—perfectionism, materialism, codependency, and addiction. But until we find the root of the disconnect, the legacy of exile will continue.

In the 1950s, an American psychologist named Harry Harlow created a series of controversial experiments which later would shape the narrative on our sense of connection. Curious about the biological underpinnings of belonging, he investigated its origins: the mother-infant bond. Harlow departed from his era's widely supported view that babies were only attached to their mothers for the purpose of receiving physical nourishment. To prove this, he separated several infant rhesus monkeys away from their mothers and raised them in a laboratory setting. Without their mothers, the monkeys showed disturbed behavior—staring blankly, circling their cages, and self-mutilating. Harlow then designed his famous wire-mother experiment.

The motherless infant monkeys were given two surrogate mothers made out of a wood frame and wire. One wire mother was covered in soft terry cloth, mimicking a mother monkey's soft fur (thus comforting the babies with a sense of touch), but had no milk attached to it. The other wire mother was simply wire, no cloth, but had a bottle of milk. Harlow found that the infant monkeys spent significantly more time with the soft, milkless mother than they did with the wiry, milk-providing mother. The babies came to the wire mother only to feed and immediately returned to cling to and be soothed by the cloth surrogate to satisfy their need for touch and comfort (love) over hunger.[1]

These studies produced groundbreaking empirical evidence for the primacy of the parent-child attachment relationship and the importance of parental touch and affectional nurturing in our development. But here is where it gets interesting: Secure attachment through parental bonding not only assists in optimal development, it informs our existential sense of our connection to the whole—throughout our lives. The degree that attachment was interrupted in our infancy directly corresponds to our sense of exile as adults.[2]

Belonging begins in the womb, where our neural network first formed its elegant circuitry, informed by not only our DNA, but our womb environment. Was our mother happy and safe? Were her circumstances supportive?[3] The moment of birth and the next few years are just as formative. Were our primary caregivers physically affectionate and close, or acutely distracted by addiction or other stressors? Was our discipline violent or nonviolent? These questions reflect a simple binary that cuts the wheat from the chaff—choices, actions, and environments that either create secure, attached functioning or not.

The public is not comfortable asking these questions. Our upbringing creates adults who perpetuate the same culture that harmed us when we were children. "Hey, I was spanked and I'm fine," is a common response. Regardless of our opinions and parenting styles, the science is sound. Warm, loving, and consistent arms powerfully shape a society toward well-being and felt belonging.

Sadly, contemporary lifestyles weaken secure attachment. Modern children experience far more time alone than in the arms of their parents. Add to it technology-creep and we have a perfect storm of disconnect. A society must radically support its parents through enlightened parental policy and offer new narratives about what babies and children actually need, so that parents are encouraged to securely attach to their children. In turn, this will help us forge bonded communities.

Research shows lack of bonding leads to increasing sensory deprivation and neural impairment. Child psychologist Marcia Mikulak examined the differences in a wide range of cultures, from the most so-called "primitive" (i.e., tribal) societies to the most privileged (the upper class of industrial-technological countries). Mikulak found that the children from tribal settings were touched, held, and carried more, and thus their average levels of sensory sensitivity and conscious awareness of the surroundings were 25 to 30 percent higher than the children of industrial-technological countries.[4] The more the children were affectionally touched, the more aware and evolved their consciousness.

Psychologist and author Robert Wolff describes his time spent in Malaysia among the elusive Sng'oi—a handful of Aboriginal people of the Malay jungle.[5] These people made up a society of benevolence, connection, and unconditional love. Like many tribal societies, their infants were carried, cradled, touched, and held, not just by their parents but the entire community.

In describing the difference between our world and theirs, Wolff writes, "We in the West know our world from seeing, hearing, and measuring what we assume to be a complex thing with many parts. We rarely use any of the other five senses we recognize to know reality." In contrast, the Sng'oi "know from *experiencing* their world as a living, organic whole, where everything relates to everything and where we blend in as but another part of that whole. It is a direct experiencing of all that we are."[6]

"The plants, the animals, the rocks and trees, they miss us," said Uncle Bob as we walked together in the Wollumbin rainforest in Australia a few months after our first encounter in 2008. He spoke at length about his kinship to the natural world. "That rock over there," he said pointing to a large boulder, "he's family. I belong to him. He belongs to me."

Our separation from nature doesn't only impact us negatively, it also impacts the rest of the living world. Even if we are outdoorsy, we may unthinkingly distance ourselves from the rest of nature, believing we are somehow different to the rock, the pine tree, or the river. What would it be like to engage with nature with no separation but with belonging? What would it feel like

WE ARE CONNECTION-STARVED. WHILE ACKNOWLEDGING THIS IS PAINFUL, IT'S THE FIRST STEP TOWARD OUR HEALING AND RECONNECTION.

to enter a forest knowing its intelligence meets ours in unified oneness? What would it be like to walk amongst the tall trees knowing that we were not just tolerated, but warmly welcomed as nature welcoming itself to itself *as* itself?

Author Richard Louv, the journalist who first coined the phrase *nature-deficit disorder*, believes that we suffer from what he calls *species aloneness*: "a desperate hunger for connection with other life, a gnawing fear that we are alone in the universe." While dogs and cats are fine companions, writes Louv, we need broader connections to make us resilient. Our aloneness weakens us just like an isolated nuclear family is more susceptible to addiction, depression, and abuse.[7]

Unless we were born in the jungles of Malaysia or some remote equivalent, we all suffer the price of our privilege. We were all, to varying degrees, untouched, i.e., denied a biological imperative to attach and feel connected. I emphasize this point not so much as a polemic in how to parent our children (that's another book), but to lift up the profound collective wounding we all have experienced—the painful separation from our existential and visceral experiencing of belonging to everything: the trees around us, the ground beneath our feet, the people in our lives. We are connection-starved. While acknowledging this is painful, it's the first step toward our healing and reconnection.

I often see this hunger for connection when people first meet the horses. They are compelled to touch and pet each and every one. And there is an almost desperate desire to be liked and accepted by the herd. None of this is wrong, of course. But it reveals to me just how fundamental our need to belong is, and how touch and belonging coexist. In the arena during the first moment of encounter with the horses, I witness the untouched adult child. We are many.

The good news is that while we cannot reclaim bonding within the arms of our own mothers, we can heal it through the arms of an even greater mother: nature. Immersing ourselves in the natural world ignites new neural pathways with loving presence. This positively influences the psychobiological effects of our childhood. We can actually change our brains.

Individuals living and interacting in green spaces report being more energetic, in better overall health, and having more of a sense of meaningful purpose in life. Studies also show reduced pulse rate and significantly decreased scores for depression, fatigue, anxiety, and confusion. Current scientific findings are illuminating what humans intuitively know: nature has tremendous benefits for the human brain, and this shows up through increased happiness, health, well-being, and cognition.[8]

But don't just take science's word for it. Look to your own experience: you know that safe, connected feeling you have when you are in your favorite spot in nature—a lake you enjoy walking around, for example? Or that warm feeling you have when you are with your dog or cat? That visceral sense is your nervous system—your heart, brain, and body—bonding.

Uncle Bob and I spoke at length about belonging, especially since it was the topic of my book for which I first interviewed him. While privilege severs childhood attachment in my society, colonization severed it in his, and historically in millions of traditional families around the world. Stealing babies and children from the arms of their mothers to be raised in missions was the colonists' solution to land rights and what they deemed the *native problem*. And today we in the West continue to steal children from the arms of migrant mothers and fathers as a solution to the *migrant problem*. In 2019 the United States took away an unprecedented 69,550 migrant children from their parents—enough infants, toddlers, and kids to overflow an average-sized NFL stadium. That's more children detained away from their parents than any other country, according to United Nations researchers.[9] Governments steal children purposefully so as to desta-bilize and erode a population. It's a kind of slow genocide.

Having been stolen as a young boy, it took Uncle Bob decades to awaken from the trauma and brainwashing of disconnection to find his way back to his belonging. When he did find it, he became an advocate for all to find theirs.

"As an Aboriginal person, you know that you belong to much more than your human family. You belong to the land and all the living creatures on it. You belong to Creation as Creation, and to anything that is living. And it belongs to you. It's the livingness—the beingness—that connects us. That livingness is what we share and what is the same in all of us," he told me.

"This livingness is what makes us family," he continued. "We are one, from the most minute, tiny grain of sand to the largest mountain. . . every reptile, bird, animal, insect, rock, and tree. Even the clouds and the rivers are our family. Some people don't understand this sense of belonging. They don't know how to feel it or recognize it. To them I say, 'Start with feeling the living things around you that know they belong to you. Those of you who've got animal friends like cats, dogs, or horses, those animals will show belonging to you. They know you are family. You can feel it when they come to you with that recogni-tion in their eyes.'"

Uncle Bob was not speaking about belonging in terms of owner-ship, of course, but rather belonging in the togetherness of connection. "Now extend that feeling to every other thing . . . including trees," he said. "They don't have the same response as an animal, because they're in one spot. But they've got that same energy of belong-ing to you. Move out from there: the rocks and water have it, too. When I look at a rock, it is not just a rock. It is my connection to all of creation. It's only our own misguided thinking that lessens our belonging, our being part of what is. The thought that we are not connected with all things makes us weak."

In other words, we need not use effort to try to create connection; all we need to do is open up to the belonging that is already here.

SPIRAL POINT

JOURNAL QUESTIONS

- What does this chapter evoke in you? How were you raised? Were you consistently held, carried, and touched? Without judgment on you or your parents, how do you think your childhood bonding (or lack of it) impacts your sense of connection as an adult?

- If you really knew that you belonged to a much larger family that included animals, rocks, and the trees, how would you live differently? How would you lead differently?

EXERCISES

- Hang out in nature, or with your pets, with the intention of viscerally taking in the felt sense of bonded well-being in their company. Let the feelings, body sensations, and thoughts of bonding soak into you like a sponge. It may be subtle; that is okay. Then recall that feeling again before you go to bed. The more moments you have of that and the more you take a moment to consciously register, feel, and somatically take in that felt sense of bonding, the more you rewire your brain to be the brain of someone who was born, raised, and nurtured in the way nature intended. And thus the more connected all your endeavors.

- Think of a question or a challenge in your life that you could use some help with. Go to a tree that resonates with you (you don't have to know why it does) and sit down in front of it. Now out loud (yes, out loud), introduce yourself to the tree. Ask the tree your question. Close your eyes and sit in silence and allow the tree to send you its message. It may come in raw, unprocessed images, or impressions. Allow it to unfold. What do you discover?

Chapter 12

Requests

Teaching and instructing others how to be with us—as well as how to be with the endeavors that we value—is essential to creating connection. You might wonder why making clear requests to others is so important. Check out how it feels when you expect others to *just know*. Inuendo, suggestion, expectation, assumption, hinting, resenting, hoping, and wishing . . . they all breed disconnection. Straightforward requests are the practical piece of the connection puzzle that link one person to another—they let people know where you are at, what you need, what is called for, and what might work for you. Requests create alliances and engender true collaboration. The clearer they are and the freer they are of other agendas, the more powerful.

For me, making requests has been one of the hardest lessons in connection. As the daughter of a narcissistic father and the step-daughter of an alcoholic, I was systematically taught that my needs did not matter. I learned to survive by making sure everyone else was okay. I felt good if others felt good, even if it was at my expense. When I finally could not tolerate a situation, I would explode in fury, leaving everyone with emotional shrapnel, wide eyed in surprise. "But everything was going so well," they'd say. Later in life, when I tried to exercise my right to make requests, I'd dress them up with explanations and justifications. I challenge myself each day to make a request in one single sentence.

Horses are stalwart teachers of making clear, clean requests. And they expertly mirror any issues that may be surrounding those requests. Below is a story of how Dante mentored a client on the topic.

Brenda and Dante were teamed together in an exercise that involved Brenda asking Dante to step backward. In spite of her efforts, Dante stood stock still. He wasn't going anywhere. Brenda kept wiggling the lead rope and making all the right cues with her training stick. Dante, ears blandly out to the side, had switched off. He wasn't hearing her anymore. She looked at me with discouragement. "He's not doing it right," she said flatly.

"He's doing it perfectly," I said. "He's doing exactly what he's being asked to do, which is nothing."

"I'm asking him to step backward," Brenda protested, her voice an octave higher. She tried the request again, wiggling the lead rope, moving her stick toward his feet. "Go back! *Go back!*"

Dante, eyes closed, stomped his front hoof to send off a lone fly. I stood back a little and let Brenda struggle a bit longer. It was clear that this was her whole life playing out in front of her—the way she felt disrespected by her family and her colleagues, how people didn't listen to her . . .

"Go on . . . *go!*" Brenda commanded again. Then she broke down in tears. "*Please!*" she begged him. It was obvious that it was no longer Dante she was talking to.

After some time, I said, "Brenda, tell me how you really feel about this request that you are making to Dante."

"Well, I know I'm meant to do it. You asked me to make him step backward," she sighed. "But I don't like asking him to step away. He may not like me for it. It's just a dumb arbitrary request, by some arbitrary human. Who am I to ask him to do that? It feels disrespectful."

"I didn't ask you to *make* him step backward; I asked you to request he do it." She looked at me with an exasperated "And what's the big difference?" kind of a look. "Are you saying you feel that you are being disrespectful to him?" I paused for a moment. "Brenda, how do you feel toward this horse?"

"I actually feel very loving and respectful toward him. The request itself is disrespectful . . . Making a request is disrespectful," she clarified.

For too many people, the idea of making requests to others is fraught with ambivalence. In Brenda's case, although she was making the request on the outside (i.e., with her voice and her gestures), her inside wasn't requesting a single thing.

Even those who appear externally confident with their requests may be internally conflicted or merely arrogant. Sometimes that ambivalence is bolstered by disconnecting and hierarchal frame-

REQUESTS CREATE BEAUTY.

works and concepts that create an outer layer of toughness to make the request happen. Some examples of disconnecting frameworks include:

- Because I said so.
- Because I'm the parent.
- Because I'm the boss.
- Because I know.
- Someone has to do it.
- Because the situation demands it.
- Because I'm in charge.
- Because someone (or something) else told me so.

When these concepts are at work, the results are not true requests—they are demands or pleadings. Who knows the difference? A horse does. We do, too, but we've been desensitized to the nuances. When a request is made from a tough egoic structure, it tends to slam into the system like train cars coupling. It may get the job done, but at what cost?

Whether you are in a military exercise, co-creating a business initiative, or at the playground with your children, the secret to true and powerful requests comes from the heart, abides inside the body, and is born of connection. Requests are the invisible synaptic threads that bind us together inside a field of connection into one elegant movement of creation. Imagine it this way: Picture a couple on the dance floor about to cut the rug in a swing dance. Before the couple even begins their first move, there is connection—they are together on the dance floor. It's that connection that allows for the privilege of requests. Then the lead makes a series of requests, which in turn engages their partner in a series of moves. In response to the partner's moves (tempo, feel, and pace), the lead makes more requests. Though subtle, those requests and responses assist the two to co-create a jitterbug, shag, or jive. Requests create beauty. They create something that would otherwise not be created. They create connection, and they affirm a connection that already exists.

In the face of their discomfort with demands, some people strategize by withholding making requests or, like Brenda, make them, but not truly. When we withhold requests, we deny creative life force. This is as disruptive as hard-nosed demands. Recently I attended a workshop with a small number of participants. It was an intimate group that was going to be working closely together for several days. On the opening day I noticed that one of the participants, Ann, seemed withdrawn—she was not connecting with the rest of us and kept getting up at strange times to use the restroom or grab a tea. The effect Ann had on everyone was unsettling and it pervaded across all of our activities.

The next day our facilitator asked her what was going on. Ann stated briskly that there were some challenges at home, but that she was here now and everything was fine. Her affect suggested anything but. Her arms were crossed across her chest, her body was rigid, and she remained looking down. With some gentle prompting, the facilitator asked her what she needed.

"I don't need anything," Ann quipped defensively. "I don't want to bring anything into the space, and so I've left it at the door."

"But your leaving it at the door has brought it into the space," replied the facilitator. "What if I told you that you are invited to bring it into the circle—to the degree you are comfortable. With that I'm going to challenge you to make a request of all of us, something you need, that will support you to be here today."

Ann exhaled. "It's my son . . . he's having a hard time at school and it's really tearing me up inside." Then she paused for a long time. You could sense the internal struggle she was having in formulating a request and putting it out to all of us. She confessed later that she already felt like a burden in the room. Who was she to make a request on top of that? "I would like all of you to hold me in positive regard, and maybe on the break some of you who are parents can share with me your experience if you've encountered something like this before. I could use some support."

With that a collective exhale spread across the whole group. Suddenly there was a warmth in the room. Ann relaxed and for the first time in two days, she looked up. She looked pretty and bright. And the group and our work congealed.

I first learned the lesson about clear requests a number of years ago in Australia with a horse I owned there named Nat. I was working with a trainer named Louise Kropach, the creator of Horse Sense for People—an equine-assisted leadership-development organization. Louise was the first trainer to introduce me to what is commonly called horse whispering (which, in its best form, is actually more like *horse listening*). She came into my life via my daughter, MacKenzie, who at the wise old age of eight declared that she did not want to learn to ride her pony (Pippa) "in the same way Mum learned to ride." Dutifully I went in search of a riding instructor/trainer who was part unicorn, part child whisperer, and part horse wizard. Did such a creature exist, I wondered? My equine world at that time was purely classical dressage so the chances seemed unlikely.

When I met Louise, it was through the metal bars of a small round pen. I lingered warily at the rails as she gave her first lesson to MacKenzie and Pippa, peering in and barely hiding my suspicion. This horse whispering stuff seemed too fanciful for my taste. At some point, Louise asked MacKenzie how she would ordinarily connect with Pippa. MacKenzie hesitated for a moment, looked over at Pippa, and declared, "With a carrot . . . ?"

"Ahhh," Louise replied. "I see. With bribery and corruption."

I can tell you this: there was my life before that moment, and then there was my life after. A simple line in the sand that defined what was—and what was not—connection. For the remainder of my life in Australia, Louise became not only MacKenzie's trainer, but mine.

One day, Louise and I were working on a simple ground exercise with Nat in the round pen. With a long guiding stick in hand, I was asking Nat to move out on a circle around me in one direction, then turn tightly toward me to change his direction (instead of turning away from me). Nat had lots of resistance to this maneuver as it required that he navigate around his shoulder in a certain way. Over time he became more frustrated and even upset. Often a horse's body (like ours) will contain trauma, and a particular move might trigger it, especially if the move engages the exact location in the horse's body where the trauma embedded itself. In this case it was Nat's shoulder. Nat became increasingly aggravated.

Seeing Nat's distress, I threw my arms in the air in exasperation. "What is the point of all this?" I demanded. "What right have I to ask anything of him? What right have I to make him do something that he clearly has no interest in? Actually, not only does he have no interest; it scares him!" I didn't realize it, but I was actually speaking to a sensitive personal issue. At the time I was in a difficult chapter with my then-husband in the wake of the miscarriage, and my requests to him were threatening to both him and our marriage. The near shrieking tone of my voice did not go missing on Louise, who knew well I was now not talking about just Nat.

"Here he is, a sovereign individual, and I'm imposing my will on him," I said. "Wouldn't we both be better off with me at home minding my own business and him in his paddock blissfully eating grass undisturbed? That way neither one of us has to bother the other, and no one suffers." I was imagining my husband and I living parallel lives as the only solution—me in my pasture and he in his. It was a pattern I had repeated my whole life. I threw my stick down and started to walk out of the arena.

I was profoundly confused by my strong emotions. I had been a trainer most of my adult life and seldom let emotion interfere with my work, let alone chase me out of a round pen. The horse would eventually do what I asked. But Louise created different conditions. Her work was not about training horses to be merely compliant. Her work was about building a true, authentic relationship between horse and human. In effect, my trauma was being reflected in Nat's, and unless he and I faced both of ours together, we'd continue in the same pattern.

Louise, sensing my deeper confusion, stopped me. "Maybe no one suffers," she said softly, "but no one benefits either." I looked at her, confused. "All of life is relationship; we can't escape it. And you offer Nat something he cannot have without you." The possibility that arises with every relationship, she continued, is the potential for both parties to benefit by the authentic company of the other. "In the case of Nat, for example, should he choose to accept your invitation to move in the way you are asking, he will benefit from experiencing his body move differently and in a more balanced way." I knew what she meant. I had often witnessed the joy and relaxation a horse experiences when he learns how to balance himself better, and in many cases heal the rigid trauma pattern. It's as if some kind of light turns on.

"And should he choose not to accept your invitation, it is not because it was the wrong request, it is simply because he is not ready to go there," she finished.

"But how do I know my request to him is right? What if I'm asking him to do the wrong thing," I asked. "What if it's just some dumb human agenda I have and . . . "

Louise abruptly broke into my narrative and asked me to look at Nat and feel my heart toward him. He was standing facing me, his eyes looking at me expectantly. I felt an overwhelming devotion to him. "Do you trust your intention toward this animal?" she asked. I nodded, tears streaming down my cheeks. "Then you can trust your request."

I picked up the stick, but this time my body felt different. Though I made the exact same gesture to cue Nat to turn, it was absent something invisible—my ambivalence. Nat turned and changed direction with ease, as if he'd done it this way his whole life, with an extra sparkle in his eyes, a sheen to his coat, and a new swing in his stride. I'm sure I had an extra sparkle and sheen, too. Over the next few minutes, we became one connected fluid movement—a dance.

That morning in the round pen, Nat grew and evolved. So did I. Thus we became true dance partners. My marriage did not evolve. But I learned that I could trust my requests there, too, and became increasingly clear and confident in them right until the end. Because of my lesson in the round pen, I recognized it was not a failed marriage due to my impossible requests, but a successful marriage where evolution (and dancing) was no longer possible.

Life is a swing dance. We are either making and responding to requests in one beautiful artistic expression of connection or we are sitting alone along the wall of the dance floor or, worse, yanking and hurling each other into some contrived, stomped-out disaster.

True conscious requests have certain qualities — they are:

Clear. They are direct and specific, often succinct.

Connected. They emerge from the intention to connect or to validate and expand on the connection that is already there.

Just. They are equitable and even handed. We keep the other in mind.

Kind. This is a quality of heart, of goodwill.

Confident. We trust ourselves; we trust our request.

And how do we respond to requests? Most of us aren't taught that either. We often say yes so as not to disappoint someone, yet fail to follow through or make it hard for requests to happen because we become defensive. Challenge yourself to be more accountable and clear when requests come your way. When someone makes a request to you, you have basically four options:

1. You can say yes.

2. You can say no (a yes is meaningless unless you know you can say no).

3. You can ask to negotiate the terms.

4. You can ask for more time (e.g., "I can't commit yet because there are others involved, may I get back to you on that?").

In the absence of learning how to make requests or respond to them, we're taught to play it safe. Absent any egoic insistence that Dante oblige her request, Brenda couldn't see the point of making one.

She had never seen the beauty of the dance. So her life reflected the pushes and pulls from everyone external to her. And when she tried to assert herself, she did it with so much anxiety (and then reactively with so much force) that, indeed, no one listened to her. I shared with Brenda the story of my round pen moment with Nat.

"What would you do if you knew that a request would build connection?" I asked her. "What if you knew that any—what you might call arbitrary—request would validate the connection that is already there?"

Brenda faced Dante, and with a sparkle in her eye and her posture erect she gestured slightly for Dante to move backward. And like a dance partner, right on cue, Dante smoothly walked backward about four easy steps. He immediately blew, licked, and chewed and offered an enormous yawn (more positive emotional responses), and then pointed his ears alertly forward at her, his eyes sparkling too. He seemed to be saying, "Where to next, my friend?"

SPIRAL POINT

JOURNAL QUESTIONS

- With regards to requests, are you a dancer (a clear requester), a wallflower (a withholder), or a foot stomper (a demander)? Looking at the list of request qualities, where do you need to develop your request skills? In what areas of your life do you need to exercise more clear requests?

- How would your life and your work be different if your requests were more clear, confident, consistent, and kind?

EXERCISES

- On a piece of paper, draw a single horizontal line. On the left end of the line write the words *No Requests*; in the middle write *Clear, Confident, Succinct Requests*; and on the right end of the line write *Demands*. Now chart yourself on the spectrum. Where are you habitually? What do you need to do to move yourself closer to the middle?

- Challenge yourself to make a request in a single sentence. Be as clear as possible. Notice the discomfort that may arise, and rather than offer more words to the person to whom you've made the request, simply be with the discomfort without trying to change it.

Chapter 13

Vulnerability

Vulnerability—an openness to emotional exposure, risk, and uncertainty—is another key ingredient in connection. It opens a door to being known, to creating a life of meaning, to connecting with our purpose and the larger whole. While we may be inclined to hide our vulnerabilities in an attempt to be accepted by others, they are in fact some of our core competencies.

Our unwillingness to be vulnerable sequesters us from our passion and creativity. It also isolates us from others. With the aid of social media, we hide behind increasingly sophisticated facades and are deceived by the illusions of success portrayed by others on their feeds. We are a society that is not taught how to be courageous, how to cope with large emotions, how to risk embarrassment, how to welcome failure, or how to look like we don't know what we are doing. Instead, we medicate anxiety and emotional pain.

Yet, on the other side of vulnerability—if we dare go there—is a world of possibility. The more we are willing to be seen for who we are, as we are, and the more willing we are to risk ourselves in the face of the unknown, the more we connect to our mainspring, our lives, and our relationships.

There's a lot of confusion around what vulnerability actually is. *Weak, defenseless,* and *helpless* seem to be the accepted definitions. However, vulnerability is dynamic and paradoxical. It has a soft side and a bold side—the soft side expresses as emotional openness and tenderness; the bold side is exposed, raw, and risk-taking. Both are vulnerable; both take courage. Gambling my entire life savings on my business is vulnerable. Telling my partner how scared I am about it is vulnerable. Damn, writing this book is vulnerable!

In 2010, Brené Brown lit the internet on fire with her TEDxHouston talk on the power of vulnerability, in which she condensed six years of research on shame resilience into a spare twenty minutes. "Vulnerability is the birthplace of love, belonging, joy, courage, empathy, and creativity," Brown later wrote. "It is the source of hope, empathy, accountability, and authenticity. If we want greater clarity in our purpose or deeper and more meaningful spiritual lives, vulnerability is the path."[1]

The emergence of Brown's work in recent years created a collective sigh of relief across every area of society from C-suites to bedrooms. Why Brown's work became such a phenomenon is, to me, indicative of just how exhausted we have become from trying to prove things every single day.

From the time we are born, particularly in America, we are pressured to be the best, brainiest, and most amazing. Some parents will spend thousands of dollars to have a consultant help streamline the process of getting their young children into a kindergarten that costs up to $52,000 a year—elite early schooling known as the Baby Ivies.[2] With most of the schools enrolling children as young as two years old, there is barely time for them to be just babies. These schools attempt to guarantee a child's trajectory from infancy to Yale and beyond, and send an impenetrable message to children—being human is not enough.

It would seem that a culture so driven to educate its children would value learning, but that is not the case. Instead, we value knowing over learning. Business schools, medical schools, and law schools across the land churn out a population of knowers, whose entire existence depends on having all the answers, being right, and remaining averse to failure. Yet failure is at the heart of innovation and genius.

There is tremendous cost to our headstrong persistence to be bulletproof. "We are the most in-debt, obese, addicted, and medicated adult cohort in US history," says Brown.[3] Like the Wizard of Oz, we may think we look capable and omniscient, but inside—behind the curtain—we're floundering and flailing about. With little to no instruction on how to deal with difficult feelings and circumstances, we spend, eat, and medicate our way to anesthetized oblivion.

> ## Horses have taught me that vulnerability also means being:
>
> - Porous
> - Genuine
> - Tender
> - Real
> - Reachable
> - Open
> - Responsive
> - Innocent
> - Spacious
> - Available
> - Authentic
> - Sensitive
> - Accessible
> - Courageous

The horses are master teachers of vulnerability. To horses, it is not just a philosophy of life, but life itself. To live utterly open, completely exposed, unconditionally and authentically themselves, emotionally porous, and sensitively responsive has been their pathway toward thriving for millions of years.

Years ago, before the idea of facilitating equine-assisted learning dawned in my consciousness, I owned only one horse—Artemis. In an effort to remove myself from the conventional (and often toxic) horse world and boarding barns, I kept her with a ragtag team of string horses at a run-down resort in the foothills of Tesuque—a tiny village just outside Santa Fe. The paddock was literally held together with duct tape and wire, but the place was happy and peaceful, and that worked for me and Artemis. There we could train in privacy, the wranglers not having a clue (nor any interest) in what I was up to.

One day I was working Artemis at liberty in the round pen, and the general manager of the resort, Ed, walked briskly past and then suddenly stopped in front of us. "You there!" he said, wagging a hand at Artemis and me in a dismissive yet commanding gesture.

We stopped what we were doing and looked over blandly.

"You!" he asserted again. "I've been watching you with that horse. I want you to do a leadership workshop for my sales team next week."

He sort of rolled his eyes as if wondering himself why he was request-ing this. "I dunno . . . some theme like *Eye Contact and the Horse* or something. Just . . . just make them sell like you make your horse dance." Then he marched off briskly as if it were agreed.

There I was, tapped on the shoulder yet again to step forward, when I'd rather hide. Ed's command was the official beginning of the prototype of the EQUUS Experience. The EQUUS Experience did not emerge with me boldly and confidently deciding to do the work; it tentatively emerged from within because the world requested it of me, and all I knew to say was yes in response. It was an incredibly vulnerable position to be in—to show up to the public with work I didn't yet fully understand. I felt naked, unpolished, and exposed. But I knew I had to do it.

For Ed's sales team leadership development day, I requested the use of the resort's herd of string horses. In preparation, I worked with them each day for an hour or so just to see what would happen. The horses' day job consisted of lugging tourists up and down the steep rocky mesas behind the resort—rain or shine, snow or baking heat. Because of this I was sensitive in asking for their genuine desire to work with me. Before each practice session, I would approach the paddock that held about thirty-five horses. Opening their gate, I would make a clear request: "Whoever wants to work with me today, come on over."

Except for their halters and lead ropes, I was always empty handed when I come to see them—no carrots or treats were used to bribe or manipulate their responses. I would then wait. Some would ignore me, some would walk away, some would stand listless, their heads low—exhausted, no doubt, or maybe just hopeless. One horse in particular, Camaro—a quiet, elderly thoroughbred with a long tangled mane, dull coat, and sway back—would remain as far away as possible in the corner of the corral with his bony hindquarters turned toward me. But others would instantly connect, their ears pricked forward and their eyes shining. Before too long I would have between eight and twelve volunteers standing around me.

Yes, I do speak to my horses, all horses. I'm pretty sure the words are for me, because it's something else that is communicated—the energy underneath the words, my posture, my tone, and my thoughts.

The whole invisible bundle wafts across the paddock to the receptive hearts and bodies of the horses.

The day of the event arrived. An hour before the workshop commenced, I asked my usual question of the string horses. Camaro instantly lifted his head from his hay and walked toward me without hesitation until his chest pressed firmly on the metal gate between us. Bits of hay hung off his long forelock that veiled two inquisitive eyes.

At twenty-four, Camaro struggled with chronic health issues, and we all wondered if this was his last summer. Like many of the resort string horses, Camaro was a rescue. He arrived at the stable some three years previously to be boarded by a Texan who lived in Santa Fe part-time. After dropping him off and driving down the road, the Texan never appeared at the stable again and never paid the boarding bills. Camaro remained forgotten until the stable adopted him and he became a much-loved member of the string.

"Camaro," I said, 'You never want to do this. Are you sure?" He remained pressed on the gate. I fastened a halter on his head and led him into the arena to join three other horses who had also volunteered for the workshop that day.

Marianna, the director of sales, arrived at the arena with some of her colleagues as requested by Ed. No one knew what to think or expect, especially me. During our introductory circle, she mentioned how uninspired she was feeling, that she had lost track of her junior sales people, and her numbers were way down. She wondered—while casting a wary eye toward the arena and its inhabitants—how on earth horses could help her improve sales. I also wondered the same, with some degree of trepidation.

The horses awaited the participants, milling about quietly. As per my design, the horses roamed freely in the arena without halters, lead ropes, or controlling devices of any kind. In this way, the horses were free to genuinely respond to their environment and participants.

As everyone filed into the arena to meet the horses, Camaro's interest in Marianna was immediate. He was unusually attentive and strode deliberately all the way across the entire arena to Marianna. He paused in front of her, pressed his nose on her chest, and then licked her from chin to forehead.

Now, this is already uncommon behaviour for a horse. But it was especially strange for shy and remote Camaro. Marianna began to weep uncontrollably. She threw her arms around his neck and buried her face in his mane. For some time, Marianna and Camaro remained together, Marianna's shoulders softly shaking as she continued to silently cry.

You might say that Marianna breaking into tears was vulnerability, and it was. But what she did next was even more vulnerable. When we later circled into dialogue, Marianna took a risk to share what had happened for her. So often, especially in professional settings, sharing feelings and exposing our innermost self is frowned upon. Revealing herself to her peers took uncommon courage. She had no way of knowing the consequences—it could create more trust and connection between her and her team, or it could provoke judgment and alienation from them. Either way (but most importantly), it connected Marianna to herself. And to her credit, she took the leap.

She reported that Camaro pressed his nose on her chest and licked her face in exactly the same way her dog Wags used to do—her best friend of fifteen years. Every day when she came home from work, as had become their ritual, Wags would rush to meet her, press his wet nose on her chest, and lick her face from chin to forehead. What no one knew, because she never told anyone at work, was that Wags died just two months prior to our gathering in the arena. She confessed that she did not want to bring personal "stuff" to work.

She criticized her persistent sadness and pressured herself to stop grieving for her dog. "Wags was just a dog," she dismissed, and she tried everything to just move on. But *manning up*, *getting her shit together*, and *pulling herself up by her bootstraps* was costing her a great deal, and her work suffered. The team's work suffered, too. Camaro's gesture cracked open her heart and invited a wellspring of grief that she had refused to feel up until this time.

Marianna's vulnerability created a bond between the team members, and the workshop took on another level of intimacy and discovery. Her actions created safety and permission for others to show up more authentically also. They took more emotional risks. As a result, the experience yielded powerful engagement, real learning, and produced new ideas.

Even Camaro noticed a difference. He looked increasingly radiant, present, and alive, and became more playful and expressive. "He looks so young!" remarked one of the wranglers. Camaro had discovered a new way of being with humans that did not cost him. It benefited his human counterparts, and himself as well.

That evening, I received a phone message from the stable manager. Could I come right away? There was something wrong with Camaro and they couldn't get him to stand up. By the time I heard the message it was too late. Camaro died that night. His weary body could no longer continue.

The next morning I entered the large barn that was empty of everything but Camaro's huge, heavy, still body. I knelt beside him and stroked his copper fur. His long mane lay tousled around his kind face. His hay-strewn forelock still covered his eyes. All the other horses gathered over the fence, watching. I stroked his neck and let my tears fall on his fur. I thanked him for giving of himself so generously, and told him that his presence had profoundly benefited all of us the day before. Camaro had dared greatly by stepping outside of his comfort zone to offer himself to all of us that day.

Perhaps Camaro knew his last day was near and so he deliberately chose to show up. His gentle nudge to Marianna opened the door to the power of vulnerability for the whole group. In return, he was seen as a healer and a sacred partner, with his own sentient dignity and intelligence—not a beast of burden whose only purpose in the world was to transport tourists up and down the hillside. That day I witnessed first-hand the sacred prophetic actualization of "The Promise," and Camaro became the inspiration behind the EQUUS Experience and the creation of EQUUS.

Months later, Marianna came around to the stable to visit me. She and I paused quietly over the felt sense of Camaro's departure. She then reported her sales were up and her team was much more connected (and therefore successful).

"What's your secret?" I asked.

"I keep a picture of Camaro on my desk, and he reminds me to be open and take risks," she replied.

A braided lock of his long mane decorated with beads and feathers hangs on my wall in my study, reminding me of his teaching.

"If we are at all sensitive to the life around us, to one another's pains and joys, to the beauty and fragility of the earth, it is all about being broken open, allowing ourselves to step out from our hardened veneers and expose our core, allowing ourselves to be vulnerable in our emotional response to the world," writes author and conservationist Terry Tempest Williams. "And how can we not respond? This is what I mean by being 'broken open.' To engage. To love. Any one of these actions of the heart will lead to a personal transformation that bears collective gifts."[4]

While conventional approaches to leadership and self-mastery focus on strength, few understand the role that vulnerability plays in effective leadership. When people are emotionally authentic, when they lean into the unknown and risk failure, when they lead with curiosity, it creates connection—not only to others but to themselves. Being broken open is a direct path into becoming a powerful leader, parent, and partner.

> ### Here are three specific practices to support courageous vulnerability in a system, be it a relationship or a leadership team:
>
> 1. **Understand the notion of *intention vs. impact.*** It may never be our intention to hurt someone or set into motion something that is injurious or problematic, yet the impact of our words or actions may indeed result in something negative. Vulnerability thrives in an environment where people recognize and validate the impact they have on each other without defending themselves (for example, "That's not what I intended!" or "I didn't mean that!"). Instead, right it by validating, amending, and repairing.
>
> 2. **Validate others.** Validate their feelings, their perspective, their world. Develop the capacity to put yourself in the

place of the other, and sense what it is like to be them. With the over 7.5 billion people on the earth, there are over 7.5 billion perspectives—all of them right. This powerful skill supports people around you to be more open, to risk revealing who they are, and to be more seen and known.

3. **Stop being defensive.** When others do reveal themselves or take a risk to share something that may threaten you or your sense of yourself, allow yourself to remain open rather than quickly moving to defend your intentions or your actions. Being open to the perspectives of others allows you to grow, mature, and become a better (more vulnerable) human.

When we don't discern between our intention and the impact we have, or fail to validate others' experience, or become defensive in the face of others' openness or confession that something hurt them, we set the entire system up for failure by pretending to be other than we are.

"What's the hardest part about being you?" Uncle Bob asked me one day while we were eating fish and chips at a small Australian beach called Brunswick.

"Pretending," I said. He looked at me quizzically. "I get exhausted pretending to be someone that I'm not, to be something that I'm not," I continued. "It's so much work to defend that."

The irony did not go missing on me in that moment—that the hardest part of being me was pretending that I was not me. In some circles this would be called insanity. Uncle Bob could not understand the concept of pretending to be other than you are. He looked at me with genuine confusion, the way a dog cocks his head when he hears a strange sound.

Uncle Bob shook his head in dismay, "I just can't imagine that. We are just being ourselves living in the moment. What more is there?"

Great question. Where did we learn to pretend? I think it was when we mistakenly learned that we are not enough.

SPIRAL POINT

JOURNAL QUESTIONS

- Go back in the chapter and reread the description of "vulnerable" as per the horses. Now reflect on yourself and your life. Are you vulnerable? What do you need to do for yourself so that you can be more vulnerable? Be specific.

- Think of vulnerability's two sides—receptive and courageous. Journal about how you can develop both sides.

EXERCISES

- Create some kind of creative scene (e.g., an altar, a photo, an object on your desk, something on your fridge) that will remind you to be courageous, take more risks, and be more real.

- Build your capacity (and the capacity in others) to be more vulnerable by practicing the three skill sets mentioned above. Challenge yourself to validate another person's feelings, especially if they are in response to something you did. Challenge yourself to be open and nondefensive in the face of feedback or when someone says they felt hurt by something you unintentionally did.

Chapter 14

Engaging the
Invisibles

O ne of the biggest discoveries people make in the arena with our horses is how to see, hear, and navigate what I call the *Invisibles*. The Invisibles are all those elusive elements within our experience that are there but contain no physical proof of their existence because they are unseen and not measurable. Intuition, presence, intention, extrasensory perception, energy, instinct, attention, synchronicities, and "vibes" are all part of this domain. When Antoine de Saint-Exupéry writes that "It is only with the heart that one can see rightly; what is essential is invisible to the eye," he is talking about the Invisibles.[1]

People who are willing to engage in the Invisibles have access to much more information about their environment and therefore more possibilities in how to respond. They work with the intangible physics that are available to them and can take advantage of other invisible influences that create influential outcomes.

Life is in concert with us and with all things as one dynamic, fluid, invisible expression. Physicist Fritjof Capra writes, "We cannot decompose the world into independently existing smallest units. As we penetrate into matter, nature does not show us any isolated 'building blocks,' but rather appears as a complicated web of relations between the various parts of the whole."[2] When we deliberately work with that concept, we leverage a power much larger than our own and access an indescribable sense of belonging and partnership with life.

My friend Lisa Reagan—an investigative journalist, writer, editor of *Kindred* magazine, and a farmer—was working in her garden one day. At a certain moment, she became overwhelmed by a cacophony of something like humming. "My mind struggled to separate the source of the noise and lower the volume. I couldn't. Everything—the earth, grass, trees, clouds, sky, was humming and it was deafening," she said. "It was the sound of a song playing: a song that made sense and was beautiful."

> THE PATH TO BECOMING MORE INSTINCTUAL AND THUS MORE CONNECTED IS TO LET YOURSELF BE *MORE* SENSITIVE, NOT LESS.

She calls her experience of existence the "one-song," the "universe." She writes:

> This song had been there all along. It was the song of a living, breathing earth. It filled in all of the spaces that weren't spaces at all. In place of an illusion of separation there was the song. It carried the seeds up and out of the soil, into the sun and air and rain, and returned them to the soil again. It carried living air into my cells. It was an ageless, omnipresent context that nurtured and loved all of life. A vibration of something about Truth, the truth of who we really are—how loved, how blessed, how cared for—drifted into my fragmented thoughts and gently orchestrated them in a way that allowed me to take it all in without being overwhelmed or terrified. Joy? Love? There are no words really.[3]

The Invisibles mend the illusion of separateness. Sadly, this realm tends to be lumped in a category many consider woo-woo. But it's not woo-woo; it's part of the invisible network of how things work. Even those on the front lines of human transformation who spend their lives in the realms of the invisible, the poetic, and the mystical, often self-deprecatingly use terms such as *woo-woo, touchy-feely, New Age,* and *kumbaya* when referring to the unseen. The message we inadvertently spread when we use those derogatory terms is that seeing holistically is ignorant and naive. We then play into the hands of the dominant paradigm.

The more feminine sensibilities of listening deeply, being present, understanding the quieter rhythms and timings of things, seeing between spaces, listening between words, sensing into circumstances, and recognizing connections are all potent abilities available to all genders. We could argue that these capacities are what are urgently required for the real leadership needed to meet the challenges of a 21st-century world. And yet, by saying these sensibilities are woo-woo or staying silent when others do so, we keep their societal emergence at bay. We ridicule the feminine in all humans. We perpetuate misogyny. This hurts everyone.

Our animal-bodies remember this ancient way of sensing. Nature is elegantly organized around the imperceptible information that moves across space. Feathers, whiskers, antennae, hair, and fur all work as finely tuned receptors for that information. The sensitivity is astonishing and essential. If a creature is not highly sensitive to its environment, it will perish. Yet, we criticize those who are too sensitive. I would argue that being sensitive is being sane. Being sensitive is natural. What is unnatural is that we are not taught how to be with that sensitivity. We are not given workshops in kindergarten about what to do when you feel someone else's sadness, or when your gut clenches because someone has tried to deceive you. Interestingly, conventional horsemanship trains horses in a desensitizing process that dulls their flight response. I prefer to train mine to be more courageous with their sensitivity instead.

When we ignore, bypass, or shut down all the critical information coming to us via our neurocircuitry—our own invisible whiskers—we become anxious. Anxiety is often a signal to listen to what our body is trying to tell us. I have a theory that the increase in anxiety disorders is due to our blunting of internal signals that give us essential information important for our well-being—information we may not want to know about (such as "this job is not right for you," "that person is toxic," or "you are cramming too much into your day").

The path to becoming more instinctual and thus more connected is to let yourself be *more* sensitive, not less. And the key to living sensitively, without it overwhelming you, is to be present and calmly courageous with all of the information coming your way. Then build more capacity to process it. Capacity is increased by deliberately feeling more, sensing more on a moment-by-moment basis. The difference between Artemis (who is expertly sensitive and uses those sensitivities to gain useful information) and Cimarron (who is spooky and reactive to all his sensitivities) is presence and capacity. That's why she is the leader and Cimarron is, well, not. Cimarron has other gifts.

There is a term in horsemanship called *feel*. It has to do with our delicate sensing ability within the dynamic connection between horse and rider. What we sense with our fingertips, our heart, and our whole body engages with the same in the horse and what they sense with us, culminating (optimally) in one fluid, interconnected whole. The same term applies to other artforms, like sailing for example. Everything you do to move a boat with wind is based on feel—the resistance of wind on a trimmed sail, the drift of a hull on the water, the direction of a breeze felt on your skin. Even though there are lots of instruments these days through which to read such information, the best sailors are the ones who do it by feel. Feel is just one of the ways we navigate the Invisibles.

Open yourself to intuition, and even psychic abilities. Stop discounting yourself when you intuit something. Stop quieting, ignoring, and bypassing the information. Deliberately notice and validate the subtle and hidden elements of life. Pay attention to synchronicities, gut feelings, and images that pop into your mind when hanging out with your dog or a tree; notice the energy of a conversation or a room. At first, you may question what you sense. You might even wonder if it's just your imagination.

When people first enter this domain, I encourage them to go ahead and just think of it as their imagination. Imagination is the gateway to switching on these sensibilities. You have to start by just allowing your-self the freedom to see without having to be right. Just like when you first learn to ride a bike, part of the learning is falling off. The more you practice, the more you hone your skill and the more you find you can trust it.

Mary, a retired business owner, was suffering from intense anxi-ety and an increasingly irrational fear of taking risks. Over time, her world was getting smaller and smaller. She came to EQUUS to inter-rupt the pattern and turn it around.

"I have so much more I want to do with my life," she said. "I used to be bold and confident. I want that back so I can really enjoy my retirement, perhaps even start another business."

Mary described herself as an HSP (Highly Sensitive Person). For me, that is just code for *switched on*. She imagined life would be better if she could only turn down her sensitivity a little, make her external environment more safe, and get on with things like normal people do. When people are not taught how to deal with sensitivity, they often seek to make their world smaller.

"I'm going to suggest you do the opposite," I said to her while we were hanging out over the fence looking at the herd. She looked at me with some surprise and some trepidation. "I'm suggesting that we give your sensitivity free rein; really open up those doors to a bigger world and let all the information come in."

"I'm already getting anxious just imagining that," she said. "Even the words *free rein* terrify me . . . like I'm astride some runaway gal-loping horse with no controls."

I encouraged her to be willing to simply experiment with this idea while immersed in the herd of horses. "Let's just see what hap-pens when you let yourself be as sensitive as the horses are," I invited. "If you don't like it, you can go back to grabbing the reins in your life." Mary smiled cautiously.

We ventured into the paddocks, me carrying a folding chair for Mary to sit on. All six horses and Kassie the donkey were minding their own business, munching hay out of the hay boxes, and standing quietly among the junipers. Our presence seemed of no consequence to them. I opened up the folding chair in a central location amongst the animals and gestured for Mary to sit down. "We're going to sit quietly for about twenty minutes, and in that time I invite you to open your entire body to feeling and sensing everything that is happening around you." I settled cross-legged on the ground next to her.

Of all the exercises we at EQUUS do with the horses, this is my favorite. To the naked eye, it seems that not much is going on at first. However, in the animal world, every gesture, every shift of weight, and every glance means something. In taking a moment to slow down and pay attention, an orchestra of meaning emerges. This is true, of course, not only in a horse paddock, but in life itself.

"See if you can let the information come in without your labels; let the things appear in their most raw form," I prompted. Labels—for example, *this is a flower, this is a tree, this is a horse, this is sadness*—separate us from the object. There arises a subject (you) and an object (a thing, an other)—the root of separation. Labeling is also a way that we overwhelm ourselves. When we label, we attach meaning, e.g., "this is sadness, therefore I am sad, and I am sad because my job is terrible, and . . ." Just being with things as they are, at a fundamental and primary level, allows us to build capacity to feel more and sense more. Instead of labeling a feeling as sadness, notice its texture as a sensation and get granular with your description of it (e.g., heaviness, pressure near the heart, a radiating feeling swims around the chest).

> ALL OF LIFE IS A VERB LIVING ITSELF THROUGH YOU, AS YOU, AROUND YOU. JUST NOTICE EVERYTHING, ALL THE INVISIBLE THREADS, ALL THE COMMUNICATIONS, THE RELATIONSHIPS BETWEEN THINGS.

Be present when you are out in nature by not labeling things, but instead by being in a state of quiet attention. When you look at a tree, for example, there is more to the tree than what you see with your visual sense. There is a felt sense, and that is an *alive presence* (or, as Uncle Bob would say, livingness). Within the tree is a presence that is invisible to the eye. The tree actually has a presence.

But this exercise is not just for your benefit. Remember when Uncle Bob said that nature misses us? The tree loves it when you give it quiet, appreciative attention. The tree is not aware of itself; it just is. When you unite your consciousness with the tree, through you the tree gets a glimpse of self-recognition. Spiritual teacher and author Eckhart Tolle says, "Nature is waiting for you to recognize it. Nature is part of the evolving universe that is becoming more conscious. And humans are an essential part of that on this planet. So when a human becomes conscious of nature, nature—through the human—becomes conscious of itself."[4] This exquisite comingling is revealed when we sense the Invisibles.

When truly opening yourself to the Invisibles, you cannot sense things through the screen of conceptualization, objectification, and thinking. While labels are useful within some contexts, they are not the whole story. It is simply a word attached to a form that appears in consciousness. Many indigenous languages attend to the sentience of consciousness much more accurately. While the English language is noun-based and it abstracts integral parts of our environment (making them into things that can be viewed as separate from the rest), most indigenous languages are verb-based, animating a thing into its complex, dynamic being.

Robin Wall Kimmerer states that in her native tongue of Potawatomi, the word for *hill* literally means "to be a hill." Similarly, *red* is "to be red" and *bay* is "to be a bay."

> When *bay* is a noun, it is defined by humans, trapped between its shores and contained by the word. But the verb *wiikegama*—to *be* a bay—releases the water from bondage and lets it live. "To be a bay" holds the wonder that, for this moment, the living water has decided to shelter itself between these shores, conversing with cedar roots and a flock of baby mergansers. To be a hill, to be a sandy beach, to be a Saturday, all are possible verbs in a world where everything is alive. Water, land, and even a day, the language a mirror for seeing the animacy of the world, the life that pulses through all things . . . [5]

As I sat with Mary, I could feel her brace against what she feared would be too much information. The horses continued to ignore us. In some way this relieved Mary, who felt rather exposed there in a chair in the middle of a paddock. I prompted her to see the aliveness in everything. "Look at the junipers and see the trees being trees; see them *treeing*," I said. "Feel all the sensations that rise and fall, appear and disappear within your awareness. All of life is a verb living itself through you, as you, around you. Just notice everything, all the invisible threads, all the communications, the relationships between things."

Mary exhaled and settled into opening herself to experience the life in the paddock around her in this way. And as soon as she did, something remarkable happened. As if on cue, each animal immediately stopped what they were doing, lifted their heads abruptly out of their hay boxes and from their slumber in the trees, and looked alertly at Mary. Cimarron snorted and spun around in alarm as if Mary had just suddenly appeared in front of him out of thin air. For a moment they all paused in quick attention, bodies poised erect, ears sharply pointed at this woman in the chair who moments before was all but nonexistent. Then, with Brio leading the way, all the horses approached her, and each horse, one right after the other, pressed their noses on her in greeting, then made way for the next horse to do the same. It was as if just Mary's subtle shift in awareness brought everything awake, and the horses felt it and wanted to honor her.

Mary's mouth dropped open in astonishment. "I always knew I could see like this. When I was a child I could see like this. I knew the world was alive. There were so many things I saw and understood."

"What's it like to have free rein of your senses, Mary?" I asked her.

For some time she was silent. Then she sat up a little straighter, and with an altogether different tone in her voice she said, "I have free reign." She turned and looked at me. "You know, *reign*, not *rein*." Then she looked out over the paddocks. "I feel like a queen."

We are missing so much when we ignore the Invisibles. We can collectively pierce the veil that would prevent us from living psychically and sensitively, from sharing with others how you once heard a tree speak to you, or how you felt the stars move inside you under a midnight sky, or how, when you were a child, you knew every animal was your brother or sister. We can feel rooted in our confidence that when we tell a colleague we just know something, we are not being weird, but masterful. We can drop into our magical, mystical, visionary, ancient selves without apology. We can assume the throne of our instinctual self-agency.

Let us walk out into the night and hear the stars speak our name. And the elk bugle to our soul through the crisp fall air. As poet Lynn Ungar writes:

> The world comes in at every pore,
> mixes in your blood before
> breath releases you into
> the world again. Did you think
> the fragile boundary of your skin
> could build a wall?"[6]

SPIRAL POINT

JOURNAL QUESTIONS

- How has this chapter impacted you? Are there Invisibles you see that you have not yet given yourself permission to see? If you did, what would they be?

- Are there ways that you judge, dull, or are overwhelmed by your sensitivity? What are they? What would life be like if you honored it as essential?

EXERCISES

- Chart your anxiety and see if it is pointing to places you have shut down messages to yourself. Follow the thread of something you are particularly anxious about. Where does it lead you? Is there a person in your life that is not good for you? Is there a vibe of a scenario that needs you to opt out instead of force yourself to remain?

- Sit out in nature and suspend your usual way of knowing— labels, assumptions, past experience. Allow a different experience to emerge. What do you see?

PART VI
Peace

Ego says, "Once everything falls into place, I'll feel peace." Spirit says, "Find your peace, and then everything will fall into place."

MARIANNE WILLIAMSON[1]

Peace is the ever-elusive, sought-after state that has ignited a multibillion-dollar industry. Sadly, the cultural appropriation by the West of ancient Eastern practices such as Buddhism have resulted in what author David Forbes calls *McMindfulness*, which merely serves to "comfort, numb, adjust, and accommodate the self within a neoliberal, corporatized, militarized, individualistic society."[2] Rather than provide a means for true peace, social responsibility, and awakening, many of today's repurposed mindfulness practices and apps simply become a means of personal control over emotions. We erroneously strive to create peace in our lives by minimizing, deadening, and ignoring sensations. Yet peace is not the result of something, but the premise of all things. Peace already is.

The only way to create conditions in which a flying lead change can take place in our own lives is to know that peace already is. Otherwise, we are seeking peace, which puts us in the future rather than the omnipresent potential of now. A true change comes from peace; it is not aimed toward it.

The most often reported phenomenon experienced within the herd by our clients is peace. Horses have an uncanny ability to project a field of peace around them. How do they do that? I can tell you it is not because they have a meditation practice, or are in search of peace, or use the latest mindfulness app. It is because of—to deliberately use poor English—*how they be*. How do we become more like them and project such a field? In the following chapters we explore two surprising concepts that are intrinsic to this potency—congruence and tempo.

Chapter 15

Congruence

I n teaching the principles of equine-informed living, congruence seems to be one of the most elusive of the concepts. I
define congruence as *a unified state of being that is unconflicted and
at one with all that is occurring as internally and externally, regardless of
appearance*—in other words, being profoundly okay with all that is.

Of all the creatures on earth, *Homo sapiens* are probably the best
at masking, pretending, hiding, and otherwise evading what is true
for them. We not only hide from others, we hide from ourselves.
We've been taught what is a good experience and what is a bad one,
what is right and wrong, and through that filter we live at great cost
to our peace. Even most mindfulness practices operate within the
context of a divided self, with efforts to quiet the mind (good luck
with that) and find the calm. Though these techniques can be helpful in regulating a stressed brain, living a life of *awakened* peace is not
attained merely through conventional secularized meditation practices. It is not something we do. Rather, it is a moment by moment
being of who we are, as we are. At a most basic and fundamental
level, this begins in the sensory level of our being—our sensations.
As writer and activist Adrienne Maree Brown writes, "The goal of
your life is not to get to a place where you feel calm all the time. It's
getting yourself to where you can feel whatever is actually happening in real time and then define how you want to organize yourself
around it."[1]

Here we have much to learn from the animal kingdom. Nature designs all sentient beings (humans included) to live moment to moment in the present, fully experiencing all, as is. This is especially true for prey animals such as horses. To feel and experience everything without exception is a biological imperative that enables them to accurately sense their environment and define how they organize themselves around it. For prey animals, the stakes are high. If a lion misses a sensory cue, he misses lunch. If a horse misses a cue, he *becomes* lunch. If horses had the capacity to reject feelings the way we do, they would have gone extinct ages ago.

We humans imagine our ability to mask ourselves as some kind of superior ability over other mammals. We've come to prize deception and masking as if they demonstrated our intellectual prowess and complexity, as if they rendered us more evolved than the rest of creation. But what we don't realize is that nature designed us to be profoundly porous so that we too might attune to all the sensory inputs. Porousness expands our intelligence and amplifies our ability to respond accurately. Open, responsive, and sensitive, we become keenly aware and instinctual. And porousness allows us to live unconflicted with all that is. It is not our conditions (internal or external) that create our unrest, it is our polarizing against them.

While in the midst of our horse herd, we do an insightful exercise with our clients that invites them to become congruent—that is, to be present and accepting with who they are, regardless of any feeling or mental state, negative or positive. We do not assist them to quiet their mind to find peace; instead, we suggest that they allow everything to be there. This moment tends to be eye-opening for participants, many of whom have never allowed themselves to be fully present—to be with what is, as it is—ever before. The paradoxical result is that they settle into profound expansive peace, a peace that was always there regardless of internal turmoil.

Participants then watch the horses respond to this. Congruence is the currency of trustworthiness for horses. For them, different emotional and mental states do not pose moral or ethical problems as they do for humans. Sadness is just sadness, fear is just fear, and being busy-minded is just that. There's an old cowboy's saying:

"Don't let a horse know you are afraid, they won't like it." Well, it's a lie. Horses do not have an issue with any particular emotional state. And they are not going to take issue with your fear. To them, it is just an element, like musical notes, or a weather pattern passing through.

What causes mistrust and angst in a horse is to be in the company of someone who is feeling one thing and acting like another. That's incongruence. Horses are like this because their nervous system is constantly scanning the environment for threat in the form of things not being as they appear. For example, when a mountain lion meanders past a herd, but is not hungry, the horses do not run. The lion is there, but they are not trying to be anything different than just being there. You'll often see this peaceful meshing of predator and prey at watering holes. The prey animals remain calm because the environment is congruent—everything is as it appears. However, the instant the lion is hungry, the lion tries to hide, crouching in the grass so as not to be seen, stalking softly so as not to be heard. The environment is incongruent—it looks like they are gone, but the lion is there. Suddenly, the prey animals become alarmed. Incongruence in the environment is what sets horses aflame with anxiety and fear.

Our human (animal) brains also jump to a fight-flight response when we sense incongruence. When someone is lying to us, or someone walks into the family gathering feeling upset but is not showing it, or a board member is seething on the inside but smiling on the outside, we sense it. Sadly, because we are not allowed to feel everything (nor are we allowed to show our feelings), we shut down an important alarm system. Most of us walk around in a state of incongruity-induced stress and don't understand why.

Countless clients enter the horse arena with fear, frustration, anxiety, stress, resentment, or sadness—any of the plethora of "negative" human experiences. Most imagine we might try to change that state, which we don't. Why would we? Instead we invite people to truly be as they are. They are astonished to discover that the horses do not flee in terror or disgust. Quite the opposite, they become calmed—even drawn in—by the congruence.

Several years ago, I had the opportunity to learn about congruence in an unforgettable way, not only from the horses, but from a unique group of people who came to participate in the EQUUS Experience. It was a Friday afternoon, and the van delivering the group was extremely late. We sat on the arena fence waiting, while the horses milled about in boredom. The van appeared around the corner and parked at the bottom of the drive, and out stepped seven transgender women, all fancily clad complete with stilettos, sparkles, and even one or two brightly colored feather boas. They made quite a scene as they disembarked—loud laughter, lots of grand gestures. Short and tall, slim and not-so-slim, and made up of several races.

To me, these women symbolized the ultimate congruence. They endured grueling hardships and danger to be who they truly are. They lived a life that required that they take enormous personal risks, lose family and friends, take medications, and in some cases literally cut off body parts in order to step into their truthfulness. Given the extremely polarized social debate about the transgender population and their resulting marginalization, I was curious what the horses had to say on the matter.

Horses read their world in a simple but powerful binary: as either congruent (things being as they are) or incongruent (things pretending). This is an amazing teaching to a culture that fears difference and therefore promotes mask-wearing.

The women entered the paddock cautiously. The horses had an immediate and clear response. Every horse moved toward them with a deliberate pace as if they had known these women their whole lives and were welcoming them back to the herd. They paused for a moment in front of the women, ears pricked forward, eyes twinkling. The women, too, paused in anticipation. For one elongated moment, everyone was silent, almost holding their breath.

AUTHENTICITY IS THE WILLINGNESS TO BE DIFFERENT, TO BE TOTALLY ONESELF, KNOWING YOU ARE PART OF THE WHOLE.

Then, the horses in unison circled tightly around the group of seven, as if in embrace.

In response, the women lit up. Some began to weep. The horses stayed in their positions and let the women relax into their fold. I sensed this was perhaps the first time some of them felt so accepted in the world.

"How does it feel to be so unconditionally met?" I asked. "The horses respond to authenticity—they experience it as safe. Your group has created—according to the horses—a powerful field of trustworthiness because of how committed you are to being your-selves. So tangible is your shared authenticity that it managed to inspire an entire herd to circle around and then remain with you."

The horses were, as usual, sublimely accurate. Here was a group of people living on the front lines of our society's most entrenched intolerance, discrimination, hostility, and bigotry. As we all remained there, immersed in the palpable acceptance and validation of the horses, a visceral sense of love began to pervade the space. What opened up was a realm beyond diversity and inclusion. Inclusion needs an *other* to include—in this space there was no other.

The horses and the trans women taught me something sacred about congruent authenticity: authenticity is the willingness to be different, to be totally oneself, knowing you are part of the whole. It is the expression of, the trust in, the vehicle of, and the channel for, love. I will even go so far as to say that authenticity is the holy spirit—that which moves through us as divine expression.

If we knew that our difference—our authenticity—was sacred, would we honor it more? Would we cherish it and protect it from distortion and compromise? If we could all, each one of us, find and have as much commitment to our authenticity as these women had to theirs, then we might discover that there are over 7.3 billion different expressions, orientations, identities—all as unique aspects of the whole—of love. All in need of inclusion. Or, better yet, no separation.

Congruence embodies
two specific dynamics:

1. **To be with our experiences as is.** This means being with our feelings, our impressions, and the sensory impact the world has upon us without squashing, numbing, strategizing, or bypassing.

2. **To be ourselves as is.** That is, to be authentic expressions of our human existence without bending, posturing, compromising, or contorting.

I learned about these two dynamics of congruence while watching the wild horses with Uncle Bob. Their sensitivities to extremely subtle shifts in the energetic field astonished me. If I attempted to sit quietly or invisibly behind a shrub or tried to be peaceful, resisting my internal state in any way, I always seemed to cause disruption to the herd and send them running off through the bush, no matter how still I remained. But if I settled into a welcoming okay-ness with all my sensations, regardless if they were positive or negative, then the horses would linger calmly. Similarly, if I approached the billabong posturing as some kind of horse trainer with all kinds of knowledge, instead of just being authentically and humbly myself, they'd race away over the ridge without me getting so much as a glimpse of them. Uncle Bob always laughed. He always knew exactly why the horses left us in the red dust.

Being congruent is a visceral thing, not an intellectual thing. In my experience, leaning into feelings is about experiencing everything on a sensation level—prior to even the label of what that feeling is (i.e., sadness, anger)—just pure sensation. Anger may have the sensation of jaggedness or heat. Sadness may feel like gravity pulling on the chest. The invitation of congruence is to just dwell in that raw state of sensation, to feel and embody it, without any need to change it.

My favorite congruence warrior of all time is author and Buddhist teacher Pema Chödrön. She writes about courageously experiencing difficult feelings, reminding us that all feelings are just energy, just life force moving through us. To Chödrön, feelings are not good or bad, but simply pleasant and unpleasant. "Sitting still in the middle of a fire or a tornado or an earthquake or a tidal wave . . . this provides the opportunity to experience once again the living quality of our life's energy—earth, air, fire, and water," she writes, reframing emotions as merely natural forces. "Why do we resist our energy? Why do we resist the life force that flows through us?"[2]

Being porous—open to the elemental qualities of all sensations and emotions—connects us to the elemental qualities of all of creation. Sadness, resentment, anger . . . all of it become a vehicle to connect us to all of life. We can, like the horses, open ourselves to feel everything, at one with everything, so that we can not only be responsive but belong. This is not about managing emotions or having mastery over them. True awakened peace lies in creating capacity to feel things exactly as they are, without the need to change them. This is true emotional mastery.

"I'm not saying turn an earthquake into a garden of flowers," says Chödrön. "When there's an earthquake, let the ground tremble and rip apart, and when it's a rich garden with flowers, let that be also. I'm talking about not resisting, not grasping, not getting caught in hope and in fear, in good and in bad, but actually living completely."[3]

When you live in this way, something fascinating happens. You access unfettered life force, you become more fearless, and you cultivate the capacity to feel more, which informs a dynamic and authentic expression of you.

SPIRAL POINT

JOURNAL QUESTIONS

- If you were to open yourself to feeling all your feelings as is, without trying to manage them or numb them, but just feel them as weather patterns, how might life be different for you?

- Spend time answering the following question for about ten to fifteen minutes: How do you lie? Just let yourself freewrite in response to this one powerful question repeatedly posed to yourself.

EXERCISES

- Being congruent is embodying all that you are, including all your feelings, in any given moment. When you do that, you are less reactive to them. Build your capacity to feel uncomfortable feelings: conjure a memory that brings on an uncomfortable feeling—some resentment, anger, or sadness. It doesn't have to be big. Now simply rest in the sensations of that feeling for about two minutes. Do not go into labeling the sensation or problem-solving. Simply feel the sensations as merely sensations. What happens?

- Throughout your day, notice if you feel any uncomfortable feeling—an anxiety, a worry, a moment of anger when someone cuts you off in traffic. Take the opportunity to build your capacity to feel unpleasant feelings. Deliberately rest in the sensations of that feeling, as instructed above in the first exercise.

Chapter 16

Tempo

P eace is cultivated and nourished by tempo—a sense of timing, rhythm, and pace. Even though amazing advances have been made in technology, its increasing speed threatens to take away our dominion over how fast (and when) we receive and process information. Tempo is about agency over the rhythm of our energies—our internal pace, our external movements, and the rhythm of our engagements—a decision, a project, a relationship. Fast is just one speed setting on an entire spectrum of possibilities. When we access that entire spectrum—from glacial to breakneck—we become masterful change agents, just like when Artemis reclaimed her throne from Brio, accessing the power of time along with her slow yet steady persistence, or when Cisco gallops like a rocket down a dirt road, leaving everyone else behind.

Working with horses has revealed numerous ways tempo plays a role in success in all areas of life: If I seek cadence within their movement—a trot or a canter, say—then I access a latent spring-board of power and majesty. If my timing is off with a request (either too fast or too slow), then I am not effective. If my rhythm between rest, relaxation, and work is spacious and accurate, then my horses perform optimally. And if I rush to make something happen that isn't yet ready to progress, then I lose my horse's trust. Likewise, if my internal speed is too fast, then I am unable to listen to the subtle cues of my horses. I end up misaligning my requests to their needs and misattuning to the moment, as well.

Tempo is determined by a larger order and rhythm with all of life. When we correctly gauge tempo with a person, project, or event, we tune into not just ourselves and our agenda, but to the whole as well, empowering us to determine what pace best serves the whole—ourselves included. Attunement to tempo creates a sense of ease and peace within our interactions because we are leaning into a more universal timepiece and surrendering to its unfolding.

The ancient Greeks used two words for time—*chronos* and *kairos*. The former refers to chronological or sequential time, and the latter signifies a time lapse—a moment of indeterminate time in which everything happens. Kairos embodies the notion that there's a right time to embark on something or that some things take time to ripen. While chronos is quantitative, kairos has a qualitative, permanent nature. Chronos is a stopwatch. Kairos is a calendar.

"To everything there is a season, and a time to every purpose under the heaven," Ecclesiastes assures us.[1] In other words: relax, it's taken care of. We don't have to be the guy at the control panel every second of the day. We can pause, we can let the greater mechanism at work handle things. Kairos, meaning "the right or opportune moment" (i.e., the supreme moment), begs the question—right for whom? Therein lies the key, for the rightness is governed by something more universal than any individual idea of a deadline.

Much of my experience with Uncle Bob was spent listening to his stories. Sometimes the stories would go on and on. Sensing my impatience, he instructed me on the importance not only of the telling of the story, but the pace in which it was told and heard.

"There are two sacred roles in the storytelling tradition," he said. "The teller and the listener. Both have to attune themselves to the pace of the heart in order that the story can work its medicine."

Larry Littlebird, Pueblo Indian elder and master storyteller, speaks similarly. "We are alive in a time when we need Story Listeners more than ever. Especially if we are to secure a continuance for land, culture, and community beyond our present moment," he says.[2] His project, Slow Story, is a video series that archives and shares traditional stories so that they do not get lost. And when you sit down to listen, be prepared to enter kairos, to slow yourself to the pace of the heart so that you can receive the gifts each story bears.

So, what is the pace of the heart? Try this little experiment: think of a ball. Now think of a cloud. Now think of a red car. With me so far? Okay, good. Now, let's try this: Feel sad. Feel happy. Feel jealous. Feel joy. Were you able to keep up? Were you able to change feelings as quickly as you could change thoughts? Probably not! The pace of the heart is not only much slower, it evolves over time. There is no timeline for grief or for joy or, for example, the slow bond of a child to a new stepparent.

You could say that kairos governs the heart and chronos governs the mind. As collateral damage in this age of speed, technology, and adrenaline, the increased disappearance of kairos means we lose heart. And when we lose heart, we lose depth and meaning. We also lose a kind of divine advantage, a leverage within our days that is powerful. We try to do all the heavy lifting, when in fact kairos would handle so much of our work load if we only let it. We can wash the metaphorical dishes, then get busy drying them, or we can let them sit in the rack and dry themselves. Sometimes letting things sit in the rack and letting the elements do the work is the best way to liberate our energies for other more important things—like rest, for example.

You cannot have tempo without rest. If you think musically, tempo is created by inserting pauses, rests, stops, and breaks. So inviting a rhythm of tempo in our lives encourages us to rest, renew, take a break, enjoy a weeklong sabbatical, or just get up from the computer and take a brief walk outside. Tempo unveils the peace that is already there underneath all the activity.

We once worked with a small leadership team of a New York City-based company. They were under enormous pressure to get the company ready for sale. The deadline created unusually stressful (and speedy) conditions for the usually collaborative and creative team, resulting in negative feedback loops within their relationships with each other. Micromanaging, silo-ing, frustration, terse and abrupt tones, and anger were becoming the new normal.

This concerned the CEO, Jen. A strong and accomplished leader who had been a CEO for several companies before, Jen reached out to EQUUS hoping we could assist her team to reconnect, and she asked if we could do it in an hour. Scott and I smiled on the other end of the phone. "No," we said squarely, "Change cannot be rushed."

We often get these sorts of requests. A company can barely afford the time (or so they think) to pause and lift its head up from the hamster wheel to create a reset for itself. They want a drive-through experience in hopes it will create genuine change. The more stressed they become, the faster they move, the less they feel they have time for anything meaningful. We do this in our own personal lives, too. Stress prompts a fear response. We move faster; we try to do more with less, when in fact the answer lies in slowing down, pausing, becoming more present, and letting another rhythm enter our lives. Slowing down in times like these can feel totally counterintuitive. And scary.

I have a lot of respect for Jen. In the face of an enormous workload, impossible deadlines, and the critical eye of her board of directors, she committed her team to four days off in Santa Fe just to slow down and realign. This not only took money, but something few are willing to spend—time.

When people first come to Thunderbird Ridge, most often they arrive harried, exhausted, and moving too fast—mentally, physically, and emotionally. This is not unique to any one individual; we are all bearing the symptoms of a cultural phenomenon of rush and haste. In the face of this, we intentionally request that people take a technological sabbatical while they are working with us. Most people are alarmed to discover not only how addicted they have become to their cell phones, but how much their cell phones literally drive the pace of every single minute of their day.

Every Saturday and Sunday, I personally take a tech sabbatical away from calls, email, internet, texts, and social media. It has radically shifted my weekends and altered my sense of spaciousness, rest, and renewal. It has also increased my creativity. This book would not have happened, for example, without my weekly tech sabbaticals.

Jen's team arrived as we expected—fast moving and wanting results. They talked fast, they walked fast. Our main job was to slow them down just enough so they could start to lean into another way of being together. Time with the horses is a natural de-accelerator. The horses live within kairos. Their decisions take time. Their relationships take time. Their movements are rhythmic. Their schedule adjusts according to the seasons and the sun and moon cycles. Just watch what happens when you put your own training timeline on a horse who still has their spirit intact.

After several hours of working with getting present with themselves and then the horses, the team set out to do some exercises in hand with our herd with halter and lead rope. In this case, the exercise was to ask the horse to move out on a circle at a walk or trot at the end of their long lead ropes, with their person in the center of the circle driving their horse forward. At first the people set about getting things done in their usual habitual fashion. They had a goal—moving the horse in a circle—and it needed to be accomplished, and now. For the horses, this linear and time-based approach was not so interesting to them. All six of them flatly refused to move forward, standing stock still, swishing their tails softly.

The group tried harder—clucking, pulling, coercing, pleading. Nothing worked. Scott and I let them struggle for a while. So much is learned in the struggle. Then Scott pulled everyone together to unpack what might be going on. Everyone was confused. They were trying harder, getting louder and louder with their horses, pushing, pulling, trying to make things happen.

"They are just being stubborn," said one participant.

"What if you did the opposite?" Scott queried. "What if you slowed down? What if you connected to them more and listened?"

Kairos is all about listening. Kairos is about pausing, trusting, surrendering, and softening. When we invite tempo into our lives, we avail ourselves to so many more possibilities, solutions, and insights. Tempo tells us when to move fast and when to move slow—when to pause, when to respond quickly and clearly. The slow informs the fast, making the fast lightning-accurate, instead of chaotically hasty. "Busy is the new lazy" is a new catchphrase. Activity is not meaningful productivity. When we are indiscriminate with the tempo of our lives, we are trading depth and quality for velocity and quantity.

The group went back to their horses and tried again. This time there were a lot of exhales, some quiet pauses, and everyone was checking in with their horse. Then, one by one, each horse-human pair successfully created a circle without an issue. Occasionally a couple would pause, stop, and the person would check in with themselves and their horse again, and then off the horse would go, circling around them. One pair, after pausing, suddenly erupted in a gorgeous and balanced cantering circle with the human standing at ease in the center. It was Jen and Dante. She was laughing out loud and Dante was shaking his mane in playful response.

Later during breakout dialogue, she shared what her insight was. "At the beginning of the exercise, I knew I wanted Dante to run his circle. But my agenda got in the way of meeting him where he was at. And the more rushed I was with him, the more he disconnected, and even became grumpy with me," she continued. "This whole pausing thing is unreal! Because when I trusted that the stopping would assist us, then suddenly, out of nowhere, Dante was ready to run! His desire to run didn't take time, it just showed up instantly, out of time, when I slowed down. It really did work . . . this notion of slowing down to speed up really works!"

Everyone benefited. The dynamic that Jen set up with Dante, through finding tempo within her partnership with Dante, and the request (and the timing of things) led to joyful success. Even the rest of the group was laughing and clapping. By the end of their four days, Jen's team had integrated a whole new approach to efficiency and effectiveness that included stopping and pausing, which, as we learned in chapter 6 (Emergence), is the birthplace for innovation.

I love the story of two suburbanites, Molly and John Chester, who bought a farm without knowing a thing about farming. Ambitiously, they bought a dry, brown, depleted plot of land north of Los Angeles, and worked night and day against all odds to restore the soil and ecosystem through permaculture into a fertile miracle.[3]

Cows, pigs, ducks, chickens, bees, worms, and 75 varieties of stone fruit all worked together in a perfect concert of excrement, grazing, feeding, and replenishing to revitalize the depleted land. Ground-cover protected the soil in which the trees grew, ducks ate the pests, sheep grazed the groundcover and fertilized the soil, chickens aerated the soil, and the wonderful Great Pyrenees hounds protected the livestock. But diversity was only part of the solution; tempo was the other. There is a rhythm to the larger natural world that, when trusted, liberates enormous capacity and resiliency. The couple learned to lean into a long and challenging seven-year cycle, with vast ups and downs, without over-reacting and rushing to problem-solve. This revealed land's connection to a larger ecosystem that in turn actively participated in the farm's success.

Tempo returns us to a wiser pulse and flow, a moment by moment dance with life. It choreographs a life lived from peace. We must challenge ourselves not to be seduced by the promise of speed and efficiency and instead tune into the larger order and timing of things that will assist us to do things better, with more ease, and more delight.

SPIRAL POINT

JOURNAL QUESTIONS

- Describe an imaginary life where your days are spent according to kairos rather than chronos.

- Are there elements to the imaginary life you describe above that you can implement into your current life? What are they and how could you do it?

EXERCISES

- Examine your internal tempo. Are you whirling around quickly inside? What image (a ball of energy) or action (a deep breath) assists you to have more dominion and cadence over your internal tempo?

- Draw a tempo map of your day or week. It can be a graph (or whatever works for you) where the high points are fast tempo and the low points are slow tempo. What do you learn by seeing your life's pace visually this way?

PART VII
Freedom

The most holy association is to
Be as you are. This is Freedom.

H. W. L. POONJA[1]

No other animal represents freedom in our imagination more than the horse. There is nothing quite like swinging a leg over an eager equine companion and galloping down a sandy *arroyo* (river bed), wind in our faces, flying toward infinite possibilities. We taste something miraculous in that moment—something out of body, undomesticated, and limitless. When we follow the way of the horse with care, presence, safety, connection, and peace, then we begin to access true freedom. Freedom as defined by equines is about expanded self-awareness and limitless possibilities.

We sometimes imagine freedom as *freedom from*—freedom from suffering, freedom from tyranny, free from this troubled relationship, free from these responsibilities. But that mindset chains us to our escape, thus further ensnaring us to our circumstances, rendering our happiness conditional and somewhere out there in some future horizon.

Or we define freedom as a bold value tied to patriotism. While that may be one valid form of freedom, the definition mires us in partisan politics, right and wrong, the gravity of which tethers down authentic expression, limiting possibility and innovation. True freedom, as taught by our equine friends, opens the door to unimagined possibility. It's that openness to a radical change of footing that sets us up for a flying lead change.

Our birthright is to be free—unbridled, unbroken. So our first step into freedom is to rewild ourselves. When we shed the ties of limiting narratives, we discover the *freedom to*—the freedom to be creative, the freedom to make a difference, the freedom to go after what you truly want. Our life no longer seems like a series of burdens, but a cornucopia of possibilities.

And there's more. Once we set foot outside the gate and gallop toward what we want, fueled by our belief in ourselves, we encounter the possibility for the transcendent state of freedom itself—a purity of being celebrated by saints and sages from the beginning of time. Here is a place that we live from, rather than a place to get to. This is liberation.

Chapter 17

Rewilding

reedom invites us to return to our instinctual, undomesticated selves and utilize the enormous sensibilities that are
revealed when we trust our bodies, our senses, and all the
Invisibles. This is called rewilding. Rewilding is the act of untether-
ing ourselves from expectations (ours and others') of who we should
be, what we should do, how we should do it, and when.

There are so few resources for us in response to our yearning
for our wild nature. The dominant narrative would have us believe
we must grow dreadlocks, wear beads, and sport tattoos in our
return, or don camouflage and hunt our own food. But rewilding
is much subtler, quieter, and more profound than that. Some of the
wildest people I know sit well-heeled in boardrooms and C-suites
or in sweats at the PTA—their alliance with their feral selves so
intact you can almost feel the hairs rise on the back of your neck
in their company.

The animal kingdom assists us to rewild. Animals model how we
can learn again to move stealthily in our environment, be nimble
against predators, grow back our claws and whiskers, sense the air,
and strike fiercely when required. Ancient stories of creatures in
mysterious and mystical kinship with humans shed light on our
shared ancestry, and by birthright as an unbridled soul. I have turned
to these tales to find the breadcrumbs back to the den of my true
wild domain.

My favorite of these comes from the indigenous roots of my people—the Gaelic and Norse. Versions of this haunting story are told among those around the world who live near the northern seas (the people of Iceland or the Scots, for example). "The Seal Maiden" (*Kópakonan* or *Am Maighdean-Mhara*), "Selkie-o," and "The Mermaid" are just a few of the names by which this story is known. Clan MacFie and Clann Mhic Codruim nan Rǔn (Clan MacCodrum of the Seals) are even said to have descended from the *selkies* (seal women) of this story.

The following was inspired by several versions, especially one told by Clarissa Pinkola Estés that she calls "Sealskin, Soulskin."[1]

Once long ago, there lived a lonely hunter. He lived out near the sea's edge, where the rocks met the tides with a harshness akin to the weather and clashed and howled most every grey and empty day. It had been two decades since the hunter had felt the warmth of a loving body next to him. The ocean had swept her away, out of his arms. Though he desperately tried to save her, she sank away into the blackness forever. His eyes were so sad. His body moved as a body does without purpose. Every day the hunter would leave his stone cottage, step into his small boat, and fish for hours and hours on the unsettled sea.

One evening, with no catch for the day, he stayed longer out at sea and took his boat around to a cove that he seldom visited. There in the distance he saw the most beautiful sight he had ever laid eyes upon. Six graceful naked female figures were dancing and laughing in the moonlight atop a large rock in the water. Their skin was opalescent, their bodies perfect. At the edge of the rock were their discarded clothes.

As he paddled, he thought perhaps he might invite one of them to join him on his boat, and eventually she might be his wife. But as he drew closer he realized with astonishment that these were not piles of clothing on the rock, but seal skins. He had heard the old ones speak about how seals were once human, and once every seven streams they were allowed to emerge from their shadowy depths onto land, shed their skin to celebrate their human form, and then return home again to the ocean before sunrise. He was bewitched by their magnificence and beauty.

The hunter was a good and kind man. But the ache in his chest for company overwhelmed his better sensibilities. And before he knew it, he was snatching a sealskin and tucking it under his seat on the boat, hoping to strand a single female. He waited.

The women danced and laughed. Their voices sang eerily and echoed across the cove like the sounds of whales. Something inside him stirred; he yearned for more than just a woman. He wanted what they had. He wanted to dance on the rocks with abandon and then pour himself back into the ocean, leaving this bitter, cold, hard world behind. But he would never be a seal; he would never swim free amongst the waves. But he could have the next best thing. He could have her.

She was the last remaining on the rock. All the others had slipped back into their fur and dove back into the water. She was fretting about, looking everywhere. Where was her sealskin? Where was her only way back home? Then her eyes caught his. "Please be my wife," the hunter pleaded. "I will take care of you. I will love you."

"I cannot be your wife," she said. "I belong to something else. I belong to the wild." But she knew—because wild creatures know these things—he had already made up his mind. Her heart too pure to attempt violence, she agreed. "I'll come with you for nine cycles around the sun, then you will return my sealskin to me."

Soon they had a child. She loved the child and told him stories of the sea and the family who lived beneath the waters. But her heart was sad, and over time her soft opalescent skin turned hard and dry. At the end of the ninth year, she knew her husband was not about to give her back her sealskin. When she asked him for it, he whirled into a rage, "You are a terrible person! If I gave you back your skin you would leave your child motherless, and me without a wife." With that he stormed out into the night, leaving her crying on the floor.

The little boy watched his mother and couldn't bear it any more. He launched out into the howling winds led by a knowing that called deep within his being. For he, too, knew the old ways, the wild ways, and his human form felt the seal-ness within. He stumbled over the craggy edges near the raging sea, following a scent he knew. It was his mother's scent, but with a fragrance closer to who she really was, her soul. Suddenly a clash of lightning revealed a mound of fur wedged between two rocks. He reached in and pulled it out. It was his mother's seal skin.

He raced back down the rocks, along the shore, the skin tucked tightly under one arm. He knew what this meant. He knew she'd slip the seal skin back on and disappear into the ocean forever. But he gave it to her anyway, so powerful was his love for his mother. At once she put it on and swept up the boy in her arms, kissing him all over. She ran out the door, the boy in her arms, as fast as she could go. Perhaps she could take him into the sea with her, she thought desperately.

But she could not. He could not breathe there. For a moment they wept together. She loved him so. She wanted to stay, but something called to her, something eternal and prescient. She had to return home. She turned to her son and said, "I will come back for you every full moon. Meet me here at water's edge. I will breathe breath into your lungs so you can swim with me among the fish and the whales and the seals; for a whole night we will be together. And I will always be with you." And with that, she turned and disappeared into the black of the sea.

It is said that her brown coat returned its lustre and her eyes became bright again. And that for many years she pushed fish toward the lonely hunter's boat so he could feed himself and their son. It is said that her son grew up to be a wise man—a keeper of the stories and a healer—who brought people to the water's edge to aid them. And then one full moon night, he was seen slipping on a sealskin and diving into the ocean with another, greyer seal, never to return again.

This story traces the archetypal journey away from our wild nature and then our return. Something is stolen from us, usually when we are quite young, without which we cannot return to our wild selves. We comply, and it is often complicated due to love. But then we find the courage to step out onto new ground and reclaim our wildish ways. Like the husband does to his seal-wife, we are then shamed for wanting to connect to our wild authentic selves (e.g., "You are a terrible person!"). I want to insert a warning here.

Neuropsychologist Mario Martinez speaks of *tribal shaming*.[2] The tribe is an evolutionary structure that has ensured our survival over eons by keeping us together. Even today, you could say that we are all born into a certain tribe or tribes—our family, our church, our neighborhood, our nationality, etc. All tribes have their rules, their code of conduct. Without them, the tribe would splinter and become vulnerable to danger. In order to remain safe and accepted within the boundaries of the tribe, we must conform to these rules. This primal collective system is embedded in our brains and impacts our decisions every day.

> TRIBAL SHAME IS REAL; IT WILL CAUSE YOU (AND THEM) TO SABOTAGE YOUR EFFORTS TOWARD AN AUTHENTIC, FREE, AND CREATIVE LIFE.

Yet in our rewilding, we may discover that we no longer want to play by our tribe's rules—rules that insist we play small or dumb, or be good boys and girls (however that is defined). Now, tribes do not like to be left. And while your adventure forth into the great unknown might be celebrated at first, soon you will be vilified because you become a threat to the tribe's safety. Departing from the ways of your tribe threatens the fabric of its sacred structure. Therefore, if you leave you will be cast out.

Sometimes the punishment is extreme—banishment, disinheritance, or physical abuse. And sometimes it's dangerously subtle. "Oh, we're so proud of you for starting that new business of yours," says a sister, "It must be hard. You seem so stressed, poor thing. I see you aging in front of my eyes. Are you sure it's what you want to do?" That's shaming. Or, "You never have time for me anymore." That's shaming, too. While the tribe will reject you if you succeed outside their rules, it will take you back if you fail. So failure becomes a means by which you may subconsciously restore your membership to the tribe. Either way, shame makes you sick by causing inflammation in your body.[3] Tribal shame is real; it will cause you (and them) to sabotage your efforts toward an authentic, free, and creative life.

If you can see the tribal shaming for what it is, then something magical happens. Our innocence finds a way back home and synchronicity aligns to help us. We slip back into our selves—our *soul-selves*, as Estés would say it. But it is not without grief. We must leave behind important aspects of our domesticated life. Often, to make ourselves resilient against self-sabotage, we must leave our tribe and find a new one—one whose rules better reflect our spirit.

In rewilding we meet our animal nature. Indigenous cultures around the world believe that we have an animal as a kind of twin soul companion who keeps us joined to our authentic wildish selves. EQUUS faculty members (and dear friends) Niccole Toral and her husband Tod DiCecco are Lakota-initiated pipe carriers. They lead people, some of whom are EQUUS clientele, to reunite with this essential part of themselves. By day they own and operate a community counselling and wellness clinic in Santa Fe, but in the other hours they journey by drum into the collective unconscious to retrieve the lost parts of those who seek their animal companions.

"As the soul arrives here to this earth, it takes on a power of nature from the animal kingdom. This is your spirit- or soul-animal," says Niccole. "It is like an imprint. They have a sacred contract to walk alongside us for the duration of our lives. A spirit animal is our vital essence that is an intrinsic part of our nature. It is a soul force or soul energy. Spirit animals are protective forces that directly co-relate to one's character." From Niccole I have learned how important it is to connect to our spirit animal because they assist us to access a wider lens, to tap into greater resources within. They act as a kind of "tuning fork," says Niccole. "They bring back a powerful instinct, a nature, an essence, a wild force that is part of one's soul essence. It is like a soul retrieval or a return home. The more you call the spirit animal back into your life, the more fully you inhabit more of who you are."[4]

The A:shiwi (Zuni), a Pueblo people remotely settled on the western edge of New Mexico, carve beautiful little animals or *fetishes*. Fetishes have always been used by Zunis as reminders of the animal medicine that a specific animal demonstrates in nature. Carved from stone in all sizes and styles, and sometimes decorated with colorful semiprecious stones, just about every animal on the planet is represented. While the term *medicine* in Native American terms does imply healing, it is not in the Western medicine connotation. It's more of a power or quality that a particular animal evokes. In the case of a snake for example, who sheds its skin when its skin no longer fits, its medicine comes from reminding us that transformation is a natural, innate process and change can be messy, but inevitable and good. Or coyote, who reminds us to solve our problems in new ways. Orca ushers family protection, and wolf can change an entire ecosystem merely by its presence.

The Zuni believe when we are born, we enter the world raw—we are naked and vulnerable. At this point in our lives, we are closer to Creator because we have no defenses, no strategies. As we age, we become "cooked"—we put on our personas, our egos, and grow away from our essential selves. Life's journey, the Zuni way, is to work our way back to Creator. When we grow old, we grow more vulnerable again; we even lose our personalities sometimes, and we may strip the outer veils from ourselves and speak the truth in a new yet old way. The animals are naturally more raw than us and therefore remind us to return to that state.[5]

You could say that rewilding is allowing ourselves to become more raw again, to shed the façade, the armor, and the props we thought we had to assume in order to survive. How did we get all those things? You might think that socialization was at work. But we weren't merely socialized, we were domesticated—or, to use a horse training term, *broken*. There is a difference between that and merely being socialized. Healthy socializing allows us to live with one another and engage in community. Cultural domestication enforces a weakening of the spirit in order to live within the confinement of consensus reality. What domesticates us? Shame.

First it is levied at us, implanted into our psyches, and then it takes root and thrives within us as an unexamined belief—a cultural code we live by without ever knowing it's there. Shame makes us doubt ourselves and hence prunes our feeling receptors—our long, invisible whiskers—that would make us exceptionally attuned to our environment, empathetic, and profoundly adaptive and alert to the moment.

Much of our work done with the horses is actually around rewilding people. Even though horses have been domesticated for about 6,000 years, this imprint is relatively slight compared to the species' previous

56 million years of wild existence. So in effect, when humans engage with horses we are engaging with a friendly, wild creature. In their company, the horses give openings for people to shed beliefs, narratives, and culturally enforced imperatives that are not aligned with their true wild-selves. In the arena with six horses, people return to raw. It is nothing short of a rebirth. Some even say it is a soul retrieval.

Susan was a high-performing professional who had spent most of her adult life to playing by the rules in order to climb the corporate ladder, leap off, and build her own thriving business. By the time she arrived at EQUUS, she was exhausted, overweight, and disillusioned. She complained of feeling listless and uninspired. "If I don't do something, my body is going to just stop," she reported, "as in get really sick, or have an accident, or something terrible." Susan's whole life had been spent becoming increasingly domesticated, from the forest to the farm so to speak.

She started her rewilding in the company of the whole herd, who were quietly gathered close around her. "What am I supposed to do?" she queried worriedly in the face of their welcome.

"You are not *supposed* to do anything," I responded. "What do you *want* to do?"

Flinging open the proverbial cage door for the first time often leads to confusion. At first Susan did nothing and just stood there helplessly. "What does your body tell you to do?" I encouraged. Finally, Susan began lightly engaging with each horse by reaching her fist out to a couple of inches shy of their noses, waiting, and letting each horse reach to touch her fist with their muzzle in response. In the horse world, this is a proper first greeting.

"How did you know to do that?" I asked, knowing that Susan had never met a horse before in her life.

"I watched them do it earlier," she said. "And so I thought that it would be a good way to say hello in their language."

With the *supposed-tos* off the table, Susan's natural ability to read others, even another species' language, came instantly online. She gave herself permission to explore and experiment, and she was successful. The result was that she not only discovered how sensitive and intuitive she was, she was able to create an instant community of colleagues.

Susan and I worked into the day, following that thread of natural, spontaneous engagement with the horses. At the end of the day, we tried something different. I brought Dante, Cisco, and Cimarron into the arena and set them loose. These three bosom buddies love to play and romp together when given the chance, and they love when humans engage in the sport, too. I brought out a long stick and handed it to Susan. She took it hesitantly and wide-eyed.

"It's not a whip," I assured her. "Think of it like a conductor's wand. You are going to direct the tempo, volume, and scope of the energy of Dante, Cisco, and Cimarron. But not like a tyrant; instead, you are going to invite—like a friend who wants to liberate joy and wild play. The only reason you have a stick is because you are much smaller than they are and it helps you expand your energy to meet theirs," I continued. "And remember, moving along with them is one of the ways you show friendship."

Leaving her with those simple instructions, I walked out of the arena. Susan stood in the middle with her stick limp in her hand. But Dante, Cisco, and Cimarron knew what was up and turned to face her, bodies taut, and ears pricked forward in excited anticipation. With unexpected confidence, as if she had been living amongst horses her whole life, Susan raised the stick and invited the horses to play with one dramatic burst of energy. Bang! The three went racing around her in jubilant bucks and leaps.

WILDNESS IS NOT A DEPARTURE FROM SANITY BUT A RETURN TO IT.

At first Susan stood stock still in shock. Two tons of horse flesh thundering around you can feel more than overwhelming. Suddenly she broke into laughter and began running with them in a slightly smaller circle, her arms waving about. "Go! Go!" she shouted along the way. For several moments the four were running in unison, in shared celebration of hearty abandon.

Breathless, Susan stopped and turned to beam at Scott and me as we hung over the arena fence smiling ear to ear. Cisco, Dante, and Cimarron turned and slipped quickly beside her, practically sliding to a stop. All three horses happily remained at her side, blowing and snorting in post-flight delight.

Later, when further processing her day, Susan was pensive. "It's no wonder the world tries to control these creatures with spurs, whips, and ropes. Their energy is so big and scary! But when I felt my spirit next to theirs, it wasn't scary anymore. I just surrendered to all that big energy—in them, and in me." She paused, "The world tries to do that with everyone. People are afraid of our free spirit. It starts when we are children . . . the intimidation, the whips, the spurs, the carrots. I want to live free and wild in the way I lived today with the horses."

Susan identified something essential about wildness and rewilding—surrender. To the mind, and from a distance, wild can seem like it might be uncivilized and barbarous. But wild is not so much an unruly amping-up as it is a gentle surrender into our truest selves. We don't let ourselves go, we let ourselves be. We relax control, and let ourselves into something larger than ourselves. Wildness is not a departure from sanity but a return to it. In rewilding we become naturally aligned with the greater order of things. We become effortlessly compassionate, gracious, and calm. Sometimes wildness expresses like two tons of flying horses kicking up dust, and sometimes it is as still and calm as a high mountain lake. "You do not have to be good," writes poet Mary Oliver, in her own call to our rewilding. "You only have to let the soft animal of your body love what it loves."[6]

SPIRAL POINT

JOURNAL QUESTIONS

- Is there a tribe you belong to that no longer fits you? Are there ways they may be inadvertently sabotaging you or that you may be sabotaging yourself so you don't leave? Who is your new tribe?

- If you had an animal-self what would it be? A tiger? A butterfly? An orca? Journal about what it would be like to reunite with that part of yourself. What would they help you do? How would they help you be?

EXERCISES

- Make a list of the people in your life from childhood onward who used shame to domesticate you. Name them one by one and describe what they did. Now go down the list and reclaim yourself (either by writing something or just naming it out loud). Then burn the paper and release the shame it contains.

- Is there an animal whose powers and qualities you admire and would be helpful to you? Close your eyes and viscerally feel what it is like to be that animal. Spend five minutes experiencing the felt sense of embodying that creature. Do it every day for a week. What do you notice happens in your life?

Chapter 18

Creation

I n rewilding the narratives, the rules, the *shoulds* and *should nots*, we can more accurately trust our creative selves: what we really want to serve, what we genuinely align with, and how we truly want to live. We live according to inspiration rather than obligation. Because our wildness aligns us with a larger wholeness, our desires and intentions become vehicles for a greater good.

Our life's artistry is found through unfettered creativity informed by presence, so that we can discern between *what we think we want* and *what we truly want*. And why is understanding our creative capacity so vital to living a life of freedom and joy? Because every single thought we have has an energy that creates something. We are either creating deliberately or creating unconsciously, but we are never not creating. When we do not create deliberately, it feels like life is happening to us—we are constantly on our back foot, reacting to circumstances over which we feel powerless. When we understand the power of our mind and become more present with the thoughts we follow and those we leave alone, life can happen by us, through us, and even *as* us.

Uncle Bob first taught me about this principle while we were riding in an airport terminal shuttle together. He had a way of delivering profound teachings inside incredibly pedestrian settings. "You have to watch every thought you have," he said loudly and suddenly out of the blue as we whirled through the Sydney Airport roundabouts. "Every thought has an energy. That energy creates things. We've each been given creative life force—like God has—to make things happen."

I wondered self-consciously if anyone on the bus was listening. So as not to attract attention, I sunk down in my seat, kept my head low, and briefly nodded. Uncle Bob didn't take my cue. "People have to realize how responsible they are for their actions; there is a consequence to everything they do," he said. "First is to ask, 'How am I being in this moment?', then it's to ask, 'What am I thinking?' Then finally you have to watch what your actions are." His hands gestured to his chest. "How you are being and what you think determines how you act. And once you act—it's done—the action will now have its consequences. You can change how you are and you can change what you think. But once an action happens, it's too late. There's no changing action once it is done," he continued. "That's where mistakes are made—in not noticing the here and now of how we are being and what we are thinking, of not being present with that or being present with others and how our actions impact them. Then our actions create trouble." He paused for a moment and smiled mischievously. "If there is such a thing as mistakes." His eyes twinkled and he laughed so loud that most everyone on the bus jumped in surprise.

As a creator, it's worthwhile to explore your values. What are they? What do you stand for? What do you want to call into existence? You are 100 percent free to make that happen. It requires clarity, a wildness of heart, and a fidelity to something larger than yourself.

Working with the horses has taught me the power of following these steps to create something beautiful between us. The horses are so present in the moment, like a pool of water—it's like they reflect pure consciousness. So there is no better companion in learning how we affect time and space to create something new than a horse.

If, for example, I want to teach Cisco to trot around me in a small circle, I must first start with imagining the scenario in my mind. That mere thought unleashes the possibility for its actualization. Then I must believe that it is beneficial for him. Without that, the imagined future cannot happen. How do I know it is a good thing for Cisco? The first way is that I know my horses love to move beautifully—when their bodies work in that way, it brings them joy. The second is that I know if for some reason it is not a positive thing for Cisco, he will let me know, I will stop, and I will explore another option with him. I have confidence that life will give feedback to me about this possible creation. Additionally, I must believe that Cisco understands me as well as believes I can make it happen.

Then I must harness my imagined scenario and my belief to my intention. When I intend for it to happen, I'm engaging my will, and my signals to Cisco line up behind it with clarity and direction. I make my request. And finally, I remain persistent with my requests. It may take a week to inspire him to do this move—or it may take six months. It takes whatever time it takes. I don't give up. Lastly, I pay attention to the impact my creation has had on Cisco.

This is not New Age philosophy. Talented horse trainers and horse whisperers from all around the world have been implementing these practices to inspire their horses into unfathomable partnership and elegant gymnastics for eons. My friend and mentor Keith Meriweather, a lifetime stunt rider, gifted horse trainer, and self-proclaimed country boy from Arkansas says, "It may sound woo-woo, but if you want a horse to turn left, it starts with you thinking it."

The freedom to create, not just as a separate individual but by deliberately accessing the co-creative forces of the universe, is a truly awesome and miraculous capacity that few tap into. The more you push into the Universe by making clear requests and taking action steps that back up your belief in those requests, the more it pushes back at you with creative potential. You may notice that I used the word *request* instead of *ask*. There is a reason for this. When we ask, we position ourselves in a one-down position with Life/God/the Universe—we are in a place of separation. Creation does not happen from a small human pretty-pleasing to a large omnipotent God who may or may not bestow a blessing depending upon if you are naughty or nice. You are Universal Life Force speaking into Universal Life Force.

Trust your heart's yearning and desire and articulate it fully and specifically to that universal source. Have the audacity to speak clearly, request boldly, and request outrageously fantastic things.

I call this the *Audacious Request*. Thunderbird Ridge would not be here but for the Audacious Request. It did not happen through writing a big fat check; instead, more complex yet almost miraculous forces were at work. My mother's astonishing healing from liver cancer would not be here but for the Audacious Request.

I learned about the Audacious Request from a healer in the UK named Marion Miller who assisted my mother when she had cancer. During a visit there I went to her house, a modest bungalow in a suburb outside Manchester. At five-foot-two and 92 years old, Marion is a force of nature. She opened the door and invited me in with a pointed, crooked finger to a doily-draped chair. "Sit," she commanded. I perched at the edge of the overstuffed seat with teacup in hand and pinned her down around this creation stuff. Here is how part of our conversation went:

"But who am I to ask for things? Isn't that arrogance? Shouldn't I just be grateful for what the Universe gives me already?" I asked.

"Who are you *not* to ask? It chose you to do the work you do. You have enormous responsibilities. You take huge risks to serve good. So by God," she said with an emphatic thump on her lap, "it needs to help you. You playing small doesn't help anybody. Why would you imagine that infinite possibilities are not yours to have?"

"But what if I ask for the wrong thing?" I asked. "What about greed and ego and . . ."

"Trust your heart. And trust that if your request is not in the highest order, something else will happen," she said. "Stop pretending you are separate from the divine."[1]

I want to caution that what I'm talking about is not about manifesting a preferred parking place. I deliberately placed this chapter toward the end of the book after cultivating the groundwork around the other primary precepts of living and leading according to ancient wisdom. We are not entirely trustworthy creators until we have aligned ourselves with wholeness through the premises brought forward up to this point. The freedom to create comes with enormous responsibility, as taught by Uncle Bob's Kanyini principle. As a part of the whole, what we create has impact on others.

> # Deliberate creation is done in just a few basic steps:
>
> **First, imagine.** We conjure in our minds that which we want to create and keep it as a compass setting.
>
> **Then believe.** We trust that what we imagine is a good thing and that it can actually happen.
>
> **Set an intention.** Our intention is like the engine; it drives what we want to create and all the events surrounding it.
>
> **Make a request.** We request boldly, audaciously, and unapologetically to Life, the Universe, God (or whatever name works best for us).
>
> **Be persistent.** We keep at it, just like Artemis did when she resumed leadership of the herd from Brio.
>
> **Be aware.** We keep in mind the impact we have on others.

The best kind of creation that we manifest, whether in our personal lives or in larger settings, is creation informed by wholeness—a fusion between our oneness with spirit, our yearning for the good of all, and our own heart's desire. When we harness our thoughts and intentions to that nexus, we become powerful and honorable agents of change. A number of the world's spiritual traditions hold in some way that how we think and what we think (e.g., our narrative) shapes our lives and the world. "In the beginning was the Word, and the Word was with God, and the Word was God," says the New Testament.[2] Studies have shown that when we tell one of our personal stories with positive or redemptive qualities (for example, maybe we lost our job, but it opened the door for a whole new career), we not only increase our well-being, but we positively influence future outcomes in our lives. Furthermore, there is some limited evidence that increasing the positive features of one's life story may actually precede subsequent beneficial consequences, rather than simply reflecting life going better.[3]

I encourage you to pay attention to the narratives you habitually entertain. Listen to a phrase you say often—for example, "I can't afford to" or "I'm so stressed." Pay attention to your thoughts and beliefs that are busy subconsciously designing your life. This is a rigorous investigation of some of the assumed truths that are either not true or are not seen clearly within their larger context. Believing that you cannot travel alone because you are too old, or start a company because you are not business savvy, or make lots of money because rich people are greedy are all examples of limiting narratives. I knew someone who kept saying over and over again, "I just need a break from my life!" He ended up in an Indian jail for years on a bizarre technicality. He got his break.

So often social change, organizational change, and personal change are framed inside the narrative of what we don't want instead of what we do want. What we focus on expands. Just notice what happens when you simply focus on your foot, for example—its presence in your awareness expands. In this way, the pure physics of focusing on what we don't want can actually create it. There's nothing inherently wrong with focusing on the negative, it just doesn't work when attempting to make positive change. As Julia Butterfly Hill, an activist who protected old growth forests from logging by living in the tree tops for 738 days, explained, "I realized I didn't climb the tree because I was angry at the corporations and the government; I climbed the tree because when I fell in love with the redwoods, I fell in love with the world. So it is my feeling of connection that drives me, instead of my anger and feelings of being disconnected."[4]

There are many examples of positive change agents who are forging powerful change through love, optimism, and possibility—Howard Zinn, Desmond Tutu, Naomi Klein, Susan Summons, Greta Thunberg, and Malala Yousafzai, to name but a few. "An optimist isn't necessarily a blithe, slightly sappy whistler in the dark of our time," writes Zinn. "To be hopeful in bad times is not just foolishly romantic. It is based on the fact that human history is a history not only of cruelty but also of compassion, sacrifice, courage, kindness. What we choose to emphasize in this complex history will determine our lives. If we see only the worst, it destroys our capacity to do something."[5]

When John Lennon and Yoko Ono wrote the song "Imagine" they were stirred by a Christian prayer book given to them by civil rights activist Dick Gregory. The idea that positive prayer could shape the world inspired the lyrics in the song.[6] Seen in this light, the song is a powerful instruction to all of us to deliberately hold the thought and intention for a better world and know it can be so.

SPIRAL POINT

JOURNAL QUESTIONS

- If you knew you could boldly ask for anything, what would it be? Let your imagination off the leash.

- List ten things you would do, create, or make happen if it weren't too outrageous, impossible, or crazy.

EXERCISES

- Make an Audacity Request vision board. Collect images, words, anything that resonates with Audacious Requests for an amazing life.

- Sit down in a quiet place. Close your eyes. Conjure a sense of gratitude and then in that space formulate one clear Audacious Request. Speak it out loud with these words: "Through the power of my expanded mind, I sit in the wisdom of my high self. I request (fill in the blank)." Then sit a moment longer with the felt sense of what it would be like to have that request fulfilled. Before you go to sleep at night, conjure that same felt sense of gratitude along with the fulfilled request. Hold that sensation for two minutes.

Chapter 19

Liberation

I f we live according to the principles outlined in this book, we have the possibility to experience the most sublime state of all: freedom itself. In spiritual circles, this is sometimes called liberation. To be free is a rarefied state of being that encompasses all experiences in one expansive moment.

When first trying meditation or mindfulness or some kind of awareness-based practice, we often imagine we are going to improve ourselves in some way. We want to liberate ourselves from thought, stress, and suffering. In my early twenties, when I first heard of the concept of enlightenment, I imagined a new and improved me—a kind of avatar who would live my life, but free from pain, without making any mistakes, and with some kind of perfect personality. Little did I realize that this vision was a subtle violence against myself, because it was seated in a belief that I needed to be different. I became a seeker and was ferociously thirsty to find freedom. I went to India and ended up discovering a contemporary sage named H. W. L. Poonja, with whom I spent an extended amount of time over several years.

Papaji, as he was affectionately called, was in in his late seventies when we first met and would sometimes be incredibly hard on me, pushing me to dark places of despair and humiliation. He would often ignore me, get my name wrong, or yell at me for something petty like arranging the flowers in the wrong spot in the meditation hall.

Paradoxically, it was there—in those states of mental anguish—that I found freedom. I had to surrender to that which was aware of those states. I had to go beyond my desire to make everything work out okay and surrender to *what is*, to the point where even the sense of *me* disappeared. This freedom is true liberation—an unconditional consciousness that does not need anything to be in any way different to arrive at itself.

Every human, every animal, insect, reptile, bird, even tree, tries to find ease and comfort. We shrink away from pain and aim toward something better. Even meditation and mindfulness practices become just a means to this end. And so we live forever confined by the conditions that surround us, internally and externally. If we are feeling okay and things are working out, we are having a good day. If our mind is quiet, we are having a pleasing and blissful meditation. If we are in a bad mood and the wheels are falling off our project, we are having that kind of day. Life presents endless ups and downs. Round and round goes the wheel of *samsara*—a Sanskrit word meaning the mundane, unsatisfactory, and painful existence of life and death perpetuated by desire and ignorance.

A much more interesting and joyful way to live is to actually be present to events, feelings, behaviors, and circumstances as they are, without the hair-trigger need to change them. Yes, life is often painful, sometimes quite so, but experiment with just dropping in and feeling whatever arises in your experience as pure sensation. See what happens. When we do this, we start to cultivate a capacity to experience difficult things and see past how they appear into how they actually *are*. Furthermore, we start to get a sense of who we truly are—pure consciousness. Life becomes more adventurous, more purposeful, and more meaningful, yet at the same time without the gravity of concern.

Who and what do you blame for you not being free, or, at the very least, content? This is a powerful question. Many people will respond with things like, "My work would be much more fulfilling if only my manager were better," "If my kids would listen to me, I'd be a better parent," "I'd be more peaceful if I had more money," "If my partner appreciated me more I'd be happier," or "If it weren't for my depression, I'd have a quieter mind." Here's the key: the place you blame is your doorway to freedom. Go there, sit with its per- ceived sense of personal limitation, pain, heartache, and restraint that it seems to give you—indeed, a perceived sense of self—and see what is on the other side when you no longer fight it or believe it.

Some Buddhist traditions encourage befriending hopelessness as a practice. According to Chögyam Trungpa, "Hope is a promise. It is a visionary idea of some kind of glory, some kind of victory, something colorful."[1] Hope puts our happiness out there beyond the horizon, in some future possibility. Hope casts us away from now—this precious, prescient moment—and into an imagined better place. It's a wolf in sheep's clothing because it promises good, yet it robs us of our life now—in this moment. "In giving up hope, in reaching a state of hopelessness, complete and total hopelessness, a sense of openness begins to develop simultaneously," Trungpa explains.[2] While some would argue we need hope more today than ever, I would argue that we need freedom and happiness now, in this moment, unconditional of circumstances.

Not everyone is up to this kind of surrender. Many people wonder how anything will get done or how anything will change, evolve, or work at all if they surrender to how things are. But you are not sur- rendering to *how things are*. This is not some fatalistic approach to dealing with terrible circumstances and events. You are surrendering to the present moment, as is, without tying yourself to the next future moment. Experiment with that on your own. What happens when you just stop—stop planning and strategizing and hoping and striving. Stop blaming and thrashing about inside your own circumstances. Just now, stop. Trungpa says that most people begin to experience a sense of peace or openness.[3] So which state do you think has more positive capacity—that state of openness, or that state of resistance?

I encourage clients to try it out for a while—to surrender to the present moment without a thought of some better future out there somewhere. Try it in the face of an argument with your partner, try it while in maddening traffic, or while the baby is screaming, or while listening to the news. See what happens. You can always throw it away and go back to hoping.

A New Practice

I personally depart from most conventional meditation practices, which for me tend to reinforce a sense of a *me* who is going to sit down and depart from the world (aka, the bad place) and enter into a more preferred experience. Instead, I just return to being as I am, in any given circumstance, as many times a day as occurs to me, at any given moment. In that micro-second, everything drops away and there is only freedom itself, even the sense of *me* disappears. Returning to that state, hundreds of micro-moments a day, is much more powerful than sitting on a meditation cushion for a set period of time.

If we are alive and we have a body, we will always know great pain and great comfort. We will experience victory and horrific, devastating loss. We cannot escape this fact. "If heartbreak is inevitable and inescapable," writes the poet David Whyte, "it might be asking us to look for it and make friends with it . . . [it] asks us not to look for an alternative path, because there is no alternative path."[4] The entire spectrum of human experience is life force. The more we build capacity to welcome this life force in all its forms and let go of resisting it, the more we taste freedom.

It's no coincidence that the training approach I use with my horses is called *liberty*. Freedom is one of the core languages of horses—freedom to choose, freedom to be, freedom to express, and ultimately liberation, residing in a state of freedom itself. As their person, my job is to ensure that state for them to the best of my ability. This kind of stewardship is always a work in progress for me and requires that I stretch, grow, and mature on their behalf just a little bit more each day.

DON'T LET YOUR DREAMS OBSCURE THE JOY THAT IS ALREADY HERE.

I trained with Frédéric Pignon, the founder of the equine spectacular Cavalia and one of the few master liberty trainers in the world.

Working with him was like working with a dharma master. Living in France with his wife Magali, also a celebrated equestrian, and a barn full of extroverted stallions, Frédéric's home reflects all that is liberty. He taught me that absence of manipulative equipment was only the surface of what true liberty work was about. Liberty in its truest form is about a way of life. It inspires the horses' unique gifts and collaboration to emerge, and it also inspires the unique gifts of the human involved. "Be the best human you can be," Frédéric would say. I had to meet each moment with my horse in a state of liberation, surrendered to the beauty of the moment, as is, without a need to change it. "Don't let your dreams obscure the joy that is already here," he said to me one morning while we worked with a young, inexperienced stallion on a simple yet precise move to take one step forward. I had asked him how a horse's one simple movement would eventually, over years, translate into doing the beautiful gymnastics I've seen his horses do. "You have to be in your reality—your simple moment—in this movement. See the beauty in that already." I found that instruction to be every bit as profound as anything Chögyam Trungpa taught.

Liberty work reveals the beauty in befriending hopelessness. As I've learned the art of letting go and surrendering to the moment with my horses, they've responded with more miraculous engagements than I ever could have accomplished with conventional training techniques. In the absence of goals, we have achieved beyond my most ambitious of goals. On any given morning, you will see us together in the arena, engaging in an elegant improvisational dance of galloping, spiraling, pirouettes, and bounding joyful leaps. There are moments of exquisite synchronized steps together and moments of utter gleeful abandon, all seemingly choreographed by something more substantial and profound than just ourselves. And there are plenty of times when the wheels totally fall off. All of it is beautiful to me.

From the horses I have learned that liberation is not something to attain. It is not some abstract spiritual construct. It is who we are. We are liberation itself. We are effortless infinite potential. We are the Big Bang and the entire universe expanding into itself—right now, in this moment. When we stop and recognize this moment as so, the horses reflect back this truth.

SPIRAL POINT

JOURNAL QUESTIONS

- Who/what do you blame for your not being free (e.g., free to be happy, free to do X, free to explore Y, or just to be free)?

- How would life be different if you allowed yourself to unconditionally accept things as they are (you, everyone else, every scenario)?

EXERCISES

- Practice this in lieu of trying to meditate: As many times a day as it occurs to you, just return to being as you are, in any given circumstance, at any given moment. Return to that state as many micro-moments a day as possible. What happens for you after a week? Two weeks?

PART VIII
Joy

> Times are difficult globally; awakening is no
> longer a luxury or an ideal. It's becoming critical.
> We don't need to add more depression, more
> discouragement, or more anger to what's already
> here. It's becoming essential that we learn how to
> relate sanely with difficult times. The earth seems
> to be beseeching us to connect with joy and
> discover our innermost essence. This is the best
> way that we can benefit others.
>
> **PEMA CHÖDRÖN**[1]

Much misunderstanding circulates around the concept of joy. Most people believe that joy is the opposite of despair, that joy is a positive emotion that results in the absence of negative ones. Joy is not that. Joy is an exquisitely refined state, one that results in opening oneself to the entire spectrum of human experience—positive and negative. If you avoid or squash the negative feelings in your life, then joy is the collateral damage. If you numb out grief, you numb joy. If you rush past regret, you bypass joy. Joy can best be described through the metaphor of the pigment of black. Black results from an exhaustive combination of a spectrum of colors that, when combined, absorb all light. This absorption means that black is also the best emitter of energy, emitting back what it absorbs. Though it appears empty of color, it is actually a combination of all the colors. Analogously, joy is the result of an exhaustive combination of a spectrum of emotions—from grief, to despair, to happiness. You then emit powerful energy. This energy is joy.

Horses express their vast range of emotion through their bodies. There is nothing more spellbinding than watching the pure joy expressed through horses in play. Like them, it is through our entire bodies that we access and express joy, yet modern life has us cut off at the neck, living only in our heads. Our bodies have become a scary place to reside, as if a dangerous and foreign land. Joy invites us to reinhabit our legs, our feet, our torso and hips, our arms and hands. Joy asks us to dwell in our hearts and our gut.

All of the previous chapters have brought us to this point. Joy is the culmination of safety, connection, peace, and freedom through care and presence. When we live from joy, we are the honorable and awake leaders who can be trusted to change the world. The levity of joy is where gravity is defied, where physics is transmuted. Then we can leap into that midair flying lead change to lead ourselves and others into a whole new direction—one informed by the ancient wisdom of the horse. It is joy that will lead the way. It is joy that will make the change—not anger, and not fear.

Chapter 20

The Body as a
Vehicle for Joy

J oy abides in our body, not in our head. To find joy, we must
abide in our body too. Being with horses invites us back to our
bodies because we see in them what's possible when we fully
incarnate. Just to watch a herd of horses thunder across a vast expanse
at breakneck speed evokes a yearning to do the same. Standing next
to a six-foot-tall Clydesdale (a giant draft horse), we feel their silent,
weighted connection to the earth. When they romp and play together,
we sense their silliness and humor. They move according to exactly
who they are in that moment, not trying to be what they are not.

But humans have a much more ambivalent relationship to such
fleshy and pleasurable expression. Other than a vehicle for our brains
to ride around on, we often see no reason to deliberately inhabit and
care for our bodies, let alone love and listen to them. Most people
treat their body as just that—a vehicle. They fuel it up with whatever
is available when the tank is empty, occasionally take it in for a tune-
up, and drive it into the ground. When it signals distress, they keep
on driving. Or they treat it as an object that must conform to certain
societal standards of beauty. They paint it, manipulate it, take it to the
body shop for nip and tuck.

At best, our bodies offer us endless inconveniences that threaten
to obstruct the speed of our lives—a knee problem, low libido, too

much libido, the need for sleep. At the worst, our bodies feel like a hostile place in which to abide—anxiety, rage, yearning, and grief. So we shut it all down, silence it up, and keep on pushing.

When we objectify our bodies, we separate ourselves from an entire universe of sensing, knowing, expressing, and living. Our body is a sensory informational network with myriad neural communication systems—cardiovascular, autonomic, respiratory, as well as energetic and electromagnetic. It is multilingual, thus speaks to us through sensation, temperature, illness, imagery, and emotion. Yet scientific materialism would have most of the population believing that the body is merely a machine.

For a time, that metaphor was useful. It brought the human body out from under the shroud of mystery and into the light of exploration. In the early 1600s, the French philosopher René Descartes replaced vitalism (the theory that life is dependent on a force distinct from purely chemical or physical forces) with scientific materialism (the view that physical reality is all that exists). By the 20th century, this idea dominated thinking in biology and medicine, in part because it was so simple. It encouraged detailed analysis of the body's mechanisms at all levels. But that metaphor is no longer useful. It's now time for a much more enlightened understanding of this miraculous living form that not only senses the world around us, communicates with us, but also carries the legacy and memory of all our ancestors.

Our ancient familial stories reside in our bones—explaining my fascination of Celtic lore, my poignant yearning when I hear a bagpipe, and my love of an icy cold and windy stretch of grey rocky shoreline. Our talents abide in our tissues as handed down from generation to generation. My gift of teaching was handed to me by my father, my mother, my uncle, and my great uncle—all teachers. My intuition about animals was handed down to me by my mother and grandmother, both lovers of dogs and horses. Trauma—ours and that of those who came before us—resides in the cells. My mother's parental abandonment to boarding school when she was a small child of six, and my father's rage from a traumatic World War II wound, all inexplicably ignite my own nervous system in certain conditions.

Intimately acquainting yourself with your corporeal landscape—all that resides in its bones, tissues, and cells from the past to the present—is essential to accessing joy. Conversely, when we treat our bodies like machines, drive them into the ground, objectify them, judge them, or ignore them, we limit our joy.

It's a radical act of social change to wake up to the damaging and limiting body-narratives, particularly in American culture, and confront them head on by changing our own carnal attitudes. By taking back our own bodies, by respecting them as the finely tuned instruments that they are, and by reinhabiting them, we begin to insert a different narrative into the world. We give others permission to experience joy, too. To live embodied—indulging in the sheer pleasure of being alive, as shamelessly as a horse bucking and leaping in the air—defies the old guard.

JOY IS NOT HAPPINESS; IT LIVES OUTSIDE THE POLARITY OF GOOD AND BAD EMOTIONS. JOY IS A PROFOUNDLY EXISTENTIAL BIRTHRIGHT OF BEING FULLY EMBODIED, PRESENT, AND ALIVE.

But we remain ambivalent, and it's no wonder. We've been literally physically torn between two polarities: we are not taught how to handle discomfort and we are not allowed pleasure. Interestingly, the antidote to violence (against ourselves, each other, and the earth) is not peace, it is bodily pleasure. In his groundbreaking research, developmental neuropsychologist James Prescott links the lack of pleasure (through affectional touch) in infancy to adult violence and depression.[1] As we learned in the previous chapter on Belonging, when babies feel pleasure through affection, their brains become wired for joy. "Without embodied love, peace is not possible," writes Prescott.[2] Curiously, the National Institute of Child Health and Human Development abandoned Prescott's research program in the early 1990s. Perhaps the notion of a joyful society as created by pleasure-giving mothers and affectionally bonded infants was too controversial.

I think something more sinister was at work at the NICHD: misogyny. A violent society perpetrates violence against the feminine (mothers, women, girls, mother nature, feminine qualities in all gen-ders).[3] Affection is seen as feminine and therefore discouraged in conventional circles. Boys are still taught to man up, take it on the chin, and withdraw from their natural desire for physical contact, yet are encouraged to engage with distortions of pleasure through por-nography. We are all discouraged from being too touchy-feely.

Here's the key: peace, compassion, justice, and equality are forged in a joyful society that is raised from infancy through adulthood with pleasure. If we want to make a better world, we need to open our arms, hug more, physically comfort others more, and receive more affection from others. Pleasure is one of the ways we reconnect with our body. If you think about it, joy is a political act.

Joy is not happiness; it lives outside the polarity of good and bad emotions. Joy is a profoundly existential birthright of being fully embodied, present, and alive. As Charles Darwin wrote in 1872, "Under a transport of Joy or of vivid Pleasure, there is a strong tendency to various purposeless movements, and to the utterance of various sounds. We see this in our young children, in their loud laughter, clapping of hands, and jumping for joy; in the bounding and barking of a dog when going out to walk with his master; and in the frisk-ing of a horse when turned out into an open field. Joy quickens the circulation."[4] Darwin would have known: his house was filled with children, and his fields filled with horses.

It's animals' access to the entirety of themselves—physical and emotional—that gives them such propensity for joy. I witnessed this one day in the horse paddocks when my cousin Brian dropped by for a visit with his wife Jules, their two-year-old son Andrew, and my mother. Andrew was too young to yet learn that his body was too short, or that his face was too round, or that his masculinity was not bold enough, his voice too high pitched, or his skin too white. He was too young to doubt himself, to question his worth. He had not enough experience in the world to drive himself ragged through endless daily tasks, chained to a computer. And Andrew had never seen horses before, let alone six of them and a donkey, and all at once.

Brian held Andrew in his arms while Andrew reached his tiny hand to the enormous soft nose of Brio. Brio blew his breath in greeting onto Andrew's little outstretched fingers. At once Andrew's face lit up with excited curiosity. He wiggled his whole body in delight, squealing in laughter, squirming to work himself free. "Can I put him down?" Brian asked, suspending the boy at arm's length over the ground in front of him, protecting himself from Andrew's thrashing feet. Under normal conditions, a miniature three-foot-tall person would never be allowed to run free in a paddock filled with horses, but Andrew's innocence piqued the curiosity of the herd, and I knew they would take care of him. I nodded, gesturing to the ground.

His feet running in mid-air, Andrew could not wait to hit the ground so he could fling himself into this forest of furry giants. As Brian released him, Andrew shrieked in total, glorious abandon. He ran from horse to horse, celebrating each one by spreading his arms wide open under their huge heads, laughing so hard that at times he fell down, only to laugh harder and get back up to do it again. To this expression of absolute, unfettered glee, the horses had a most curious response. They surrounded him, nearly stooping, keeping their heads low and ears forward as if trying to make themselves small for Andrew. Their eyes were twinkling in gentle humor. It was as if the most precious creature on earth were amongst them.

Like sympathetic strings on a musical instrument, the horses resonated with this pure state of joy. They began delicately, softly, carefully, but jubilantly swirling and moving around Andrew in a shared dance of elation. For several minutes Andrew and the horses delighted in each other's company, Andrew running and laughing, arms spread, the horses following him around with their lowered heads, crouched bodies, and twinkling eyes. The adults in the paddock had little significance. All we could do was roar with laughter to witness this spectacle of pure joy. It was a moment I will never forget.

I want to live like that. I want to run with abandon amongst all that amazes me and fling myself into all of it without hesitation. How do we become more like Andrew amongst the horses? One specific condition was at play in this scenario to support that joyful moment: trust. Because a field of trust was created by the horses (and my trust in them), Jules and Brian departed from the usual parental concern and instead allowed Andrew the freedom to express himself.

They could have easily (and understandably) squashed the moment and refused to release Andrew into the great unknown. Joy is the byproduct of leaping into that unknown—trusting life, trusting ourselves.

Living a life of joy is the result of three essential practices:

Trusting the unknown. A life guided by fear is a joyless life.

Accepting and experiencing all emotions, good and bad. We explored this in chapter 15. I have a loved one in my life who has suffered from severe depression since childhood. Yet she is one of the most magnetic, radiant, caring, spontaneous, and joyful people I've ever met. One day I described my experience of her and asked her how she does it. "I've learned to be wide open to all my experiences and stop fighting the depression," she responded. "Joy doesn't bypass my depression; it includes it."

Practicing radical self-care. What is self-care exactly? It's much more than doing yoga now and again, or eating well. Self-care ensures that our daily practices, habits, and rituals keep us emotionally, physically, mentally, and spiritually vital so that we can live full, creative, and joyful lives and be of service to others.

In countless surveys that EQUUS has conducted of high-performing professionals at the peak of their game, lack of self-care was the number one reason cited as to why they felt they had plateaued. One of the leading edges of human evolution and transformation has to do with our embodied return to ourselves through the practical action steps of self-care habits. Taking care of our bodies is not a selfish, individualized process—when we inhabit our physical selves, we inhabit the world. As author of *Pleasure Activism*, Adrienne Maree Brown says, "I don't think we can really feel for the collective if we can't feel ourselves."[5]

Below is the EQUUS self-care survey we give to our clients, all of whom aspire to do courageous and innovative things in the world. Some of the questions are predictable, some are surprising. Take yourself through the list below and see how you fare.

EQUUS Self-Care Profile™

Rate yourself for each statement based on the following scale:

Never (1)

Almost Never (2)

Sometimes (3)

Almost Always (4)

Always (5)

BODY

I eat a meal or snack approximately every three hours throughout the day.

I drink plenty of water throughout the day.

I exercise on a regular basis, regardless of my circumstances.

I eat foods that keep my body vital and strong and avoid foods that diminish my energy.

I get seven to eight hours of sleep per night and practice good sleep hygiene.

I recognize my body is a multilingual sensory system that communicates in many ways and listens in many ways.

I listen to my body and its cues, and adjust my life habits accordingly in order to support my health.

I love my body and my appearance, and I am resilient against narratives of the ideas of a "perfect" body size, shape, and age.

I take care of my physical appearance, including the clothes I wear and the way I move through the world.

I receive massages regularly.

EMOTION

I know how to regulate myself and others in times of stress.

I know what brings me joy, pleasure, and happiness.

I engage in activities that bring me joy, pleasure, and happiness.

I respond to emotional confrontation in a skillful way.

I have a high level of positive emotional energy in my life.

I am comfortable with vulnerability—in others and in myself.

ENERGY

My living and working environments are tidy and beautiful.

I keep my life free of clutter and unnecessary material baggage.

I surround myself with good, wise company and friends and colleagues that inspire me, support me, and challenge me.

I challenge myself by leaping into the unknown. I also want others to challenge me.

I am kind to myself—physically, emotionally, mentally, and spiritually.

I take regular breaks from technology.

I do not task-load my days.

I pay attention to what gives me energy and what depletes my energy.

I do not waste my time and energy on life-depleting relationships.

I keep the energy between myself and my relationships clean, honest, and clear. If something needs to be addressed, I address it quickly and don't let it linger.

I am selective about where I invest my energy and time.

MIND

I accept criticism and feedback gracefully and nondefensively.

I sustain attention for long periods of time.

I have strategies in place for focusing in certain situations so that emails, calls, or other disruptions are eliminated or minimized.

I am honest with myself even when it's difficult.

I take a learner's or a player's mindset instead of a victim mindset.

SPIRIT

I am guided more by internal vision than by external pressures.

What I say and do is a reflection of my purpose and my values.

I have a clear sense of what my values are, and I live within them.

I am affectionate with others; touch and affection are a regular part of my day.

I am touched, hugged, and held on a daily basis.

I have specific rituals, routines, spiritual practices, and habits that enable me to rest, recharge, and be inspired and fulfilled.

I ask for help.

I am able to receive care, compliments, support, credit, and positive feedback.

I sing and/or dance.

Add up your score and divide the total number by 41. Your number is the average score.

IF YOUR AVERAGE SCORE IS:

1.0–2.0

It looks like you are giving a bare minimum to your body and your well-being. Perhaps you don't think self-care matters, or you are operating under some limiting beliefs around your worth. This will have long-term negative impacts on your performance, creativity, and fulfillment. A change is needed before the negative consequences catch up with you.

2.1–3.0

You do okay at taking care of yourself sometimes, but you are not consistent, or you do not cover enough areas of your life—mental, emotional, physical, and spiritual. What area(s) are you neglecting and why? Or what is the belief behind only attending to your well-being sometimes? What you put into self-care will show the same results in the rest of your life.

3.1–4.0

Great work! Self-care is not an easy thing to say yes to, and it looks like you are well on your way to creating a solid foundation for yourself in many areas of your life. Are there some places you can improve? Are there areas in your well-being practices that have been ignored or that you still have not made time for? The difference between good and great is right at this line. If you give the best to yourself, you get the best out of yourself.

4.1–5.0

Congratulations! You embrace yourself, your worth, and your well-being. Chances are others feel really good around you too. You are a high performer and create amazing outcomes in your life, and because of your continued self-care, there awaits a world of possibilities for you. What more do you want to achieve for yourself?

HERE ARE SOME QUESTIONS
TO CONSIDER:

Did you learn anything new about yourself through this profile?

Did you learn anything new about self-care through this profile?

Where might there be a weak link in your self-care?

What does that weak link cost you? Your dreams and ambitions?

What can you do to take your self-care to the next level?

Some of the questions in the profile are what we might predict around our idea of self-care. But some might be surprising. For example, why is vulnerability linked to self-care? Studies show that vulnerability builds intimacy (thus keeping away loneliness) and increases self-worth, accountability, and trust (thus creating better outcomes in your life).

And then there's that question about singing and dancing. We have been doing both since the beginning of time. The thousands-year-old iconic god-figure of Nataraja dances across caves in India. We've done it forever because it has significance to our bodies and our well-being—social, spiritual, and personal. Recent studies point to significant positive neurological effects of dancing. In one telling article in *Scientific American*, a neuroscientist at Columbia University posits that dance stimulates the brain's reward centers and activates its sensory and motor circuits.[6] Another study at the Albert Einstein College of Medicine suggests that dance improves brain health. The researchers investigated the effect leisure activities (e.g., cycling, golfing, swimming, and playing tennis) had on the elderly. As it turns out, of all the activities studied, only dancing lowered participants' risk of dementia.[7]

Animals and children dance instinctually without ever seeing another person do it. Sadly, modern American culture has made dancing less accessible or a couples-only thing, relegating it to nightclubs or to those who refine their skill to specific styles (salsa or swing, for example). All this is wonderful, but it leaves much of the population off the dance floor. We need to open our public spaces more to dance—freestyle—just for the fun of it, for all ages from 2 to 102.

Singing, too, activates reward centers in the brain, releasing endorphins and oxytocin. And group singing is exhilarating and even transformative. Studies have shown that singing enhances feelings of trust and bonding and reduces depression and loneliness.[8]

After answering the EQUUS Self-Care Profile questions, I invite you to explore which aspects are missing in your life. Then embed more practices, rituals, and habits that create a dynamic system of truly caring for yourself. As Audre Lorde, New York's poet laureate (1991–1993) and self-described "black lesbian feminist warrior mother" writes, "Caring for myself is not self-indulgence. It is self-preservation, and that is an act of political warfare."[9]

While we can't make ourselves feel joy, we can create conditions in our lives that make joy more available. Often it is as simple as removing the unnecessary layers that obstruct it—layers we took on because we thought it might be a good idea, or believed they might protect us, or hoped would make us more successful. The layers are simply unexamined beliefs we inherited. Joy is your birthright, your original nature, intrinsic to your incarnation. Joy is transcendental, as well as grounded. As you'll see in the final chapter of this book, joy is not some fluffy, feel-good indulgence to be dismissed. It is a defiant, formidable influence. It is the lift-off for your flying lead change.

SPIRAL POINT

JOURNAL QUESTIONS

- Has this chapter changed the way you think about your body and your self-care? If so, how?

- Take a few moments to imagine your body sitting in a chair in front of you. If it could talk to you, what would it say? Write it all down.

EXERCISES

- Draw an outline of your body on a piece of paper. Now with crayons or colored pencil, map out all the various sensations that you feel from your toes all the way up to your head. You might make a color or shape correlate to a specific sensation, memory, or gift that you have. What was it like to viscerally explore your body that way?

- Complete the EQUUS Self-Care Profile. What did you learn? What are some actions steps you can commit to doing in the next seven days that will support you to have an improved self-care profile?

Chapter 21

Leading the Flying Change

T ogether we've travelled the full arc of wisdom as taught
by our ancient equine companions: care, presence, safety,
connection, peace, and freedom. Living inside that wisdom
culminates in joy—the zenith of the other six precepts. It may
seem like a surprising conclusion. It may seem frivolous. But joy
is an indomitable lion. It brings a radical capacity for profound
change in our lives and in the world. And although joy is placed at
the end of this book, it is actually just the beginning of a new way
forward. From joy, we can attend to our relationships, our leadership, and our activism and move out into the world as a pure and
invincible force for good. I would argue that until we live from joy,
we can get nothing of transformational substance done. What element has been missing from our organizational, political, and social
change? Joy.

We are in a time when we are called to do courageous things, not
just on behalf of our country, or our gender, or race, but on behalf of
our planet—every plant and animal and our entire humanity. As the
Zapatistas say, "We're trying to build a world in which many worlds
fit."[1] We are at a civilizational crossroads: in the time of the Great
Outwaiting. What will we choose? Fear or love? If love is what we
want to choose, then joy will make it happen, moment by moment.

As social justice activist Brittany Packnett writes, "Joy is a break from a news cycle that will discombobulate me if I let it. Joy is a middle finger to a bigot with a torch who wants to see me cower. Joy is a moral victory against extremism and a political win, fueling us to persist and resist. Joy is resistance to the hate that fills the front page."[2] Joy is fundamentally different than turning a blind eye.

In my early twenties (back when I was prone to more youthful reactivity than mature responsiveness), I aligned myself with some pretty extreme activists—Earth First, PETA, Greenpeace, and other outspoken organizations on the front lines of birth rights, human rights, and minority rights. At the time it seemed that outrage and negative dramatic exaggeration of facts was the fuel that would shake a sleeping

I DO NOT BELIEVE THAT WE EMPOWER SOCIAL CHANGE BY SHAMING, TERRIFYING, BULLYING, OR SCARING PEOPLE WITH FRIGHTENING AND HYPERBOLIC MESSAGING.

society out of its stupor. But that came at a cost to us and to the causes for which we fought. Joy, pleasure, and happiness was the collateral damage of a life lived in service.

It's interesting to note that joy is systematically and deliberately stripped away by structures that wish to disempower those who would speak out against it. In extreme cases such as autocratic regimes, forms of joy are banned. Dictators know that joy has a galvanic and unifying force, and that anything that gathers and channels that energy threatens to upend the rigid control of a population. So when we deny ourselves joy, we are inadvertently playing into the hands of oppression. A joyless life is the result of internalized homophobia, internalized racism, sexism, ageism—internalized shame. Joy is the great energizer for change and counters the rigidity of oppressive structures in a nonviolent way.

I depart from the presumption that we need to use rage and fear as tactics for social change. I do not believe that we empower social change by shaming, terrifying, bullying, or scaring people with frightening and hyperbolic messaging. Facts are important; when we embellish them for our own agenda (even one that is noble) we render the public immobile with fear and undermine our integrity. Rejecting someone for their beliefs creates more division. Shaming a gender or race for behaving badly toward another gender or race creates more toxicity. The collateral with all these approaches is joy—the superpower we need to lift us out of our civilizational predicament.

I don't take a moral stand against using fear, rage, and shame to provoke people into action. It's just that from a brain-behavioral point of view, it's ineffective. When we use finger-wagging words that arouse fear or we threaten with anger or even use words that evoke obligation (like *should, must, need to, have to*), we immediately push the brains of our audience into a fight-flight-freeze response. A brain cannot be innovative, compassionate, or wise when it is intimidated.

The only way to ensure that we access the most collective wisdom and creativity possible is to create conditions of safety, peace, connection, and freedom through care and presence—just as the horses do—and then lead from the resulting joy. We will then inspire change, instead of conspiring against that which we want to change. "The trouble is that we have a bad habit, encouraged by pedants and sophisticates: considering happiness as something rather stupid," states author Ursula K. Le Guin. "Only pain is intellectual, only evil interesting. This is the treason of the artists; a refusal to admit the banality of evil and the terrible boredom of pain."[3]

At EQUUS, we donate our meeting venue and learning campus at Thunderbird Ridge to a local multicultural and multiracial organization founded and led by Native women called Tewa Women United for some of their elder meetings. Founded in 1989 as a support group for women from the Pueblos of northern New Mexico, Tewa Women United concerns itself with the traumatic effects of colonization, religious inquisition, and militarization leading to issues such as alcoholism, suicide, domestic/sexual violence, and environmental violence. In the safe space they create, they transform and empower one another through critical analysis and by embracing and reaffirming their cultural identity. Their mission is to end "all forms of violence against Native women and girls, Mother Earth, and to promote peace in New Mexico."[4]

When the elders—the *sayas*—arrive at Thunderbird Ridge, it is my and Scott's cue to disappear once we greet them so that they can attend to their important business. Afterward, they often invite us to share some watermelon or a bowl of homemade hot beans, which we enthusiastically accept, because it is an opportunity to sit with the sayas and hear a story or some relevant piece of wisdom.

One day we were looking out over the horse paddocks together, me nibbling on an offered peach. A younger member of the group was speaking about the #MeToo movement. She was musing about the famous men appearing in the headlines, as well as other men she knew who were behaving badly, and she proclaimed the importance of calling them out. I nodded in stalwart agreement. But out of the corner of my eye I saw one of the sayas shaking her head slowly. Small-framed, with a beautiful ancient face in which every line revealed the twists and turns in her long life, she sat quietly for a moment. Her pause pulled us in like planets around a sun. "We need to call them *in*, not call them out," she said quietly.

She was right. Calling the other in is inclusive, and far more effective than shaming and blaming. Joy calls in. Joy attracts; joy compels. It unifies and heals.

Being the change means being joyful, if the change we want to enact does, in fact, ultimately include joy for all. The state of joyousness is the activism itself. This is not spiritual bypassing; it is not donning rose-colored glasses and being happy in spite of the horror. No, we are taking in the horror, daring to feel it fully, and then choosing to come fully and passionately alive and shine into the darkness. Though this is a paradoxical response to darkness, it unleashes a total paradigm shift—a new way, an entirely different dimension.

Sadly, the definition of joy has been culturally appropriated by greeting card companies and New Age apps. We are led to believe joy is about gaiety—the result of all things going splendidly. But joy is a sublime and nuanced spiritual state that can appear as much cool, quiet, and surrendered as jubilant and bright. Joy is elemental—not merely emotional. So joy takes on a spiritual capacity that is at the same time grounded here on earth. Hence it is what can leverage miraculous changes in the physical realm. Joy is the conduit between heaven and earth.

Of all the lessons horses have taught me, joy is perhaps the most illuminating. My role as their person, their leader, is to perpetuate their biological imperative and propensity for joy. This means that I must create conditions of safety, connection, peace, and freedom through my care and presence. It is both a professional endeavor and a spiritual practice. Each day, every minute, they reflect to me how well I am doing that. Our horses are either joyful, or not. They always tell the truth. And there is no intimidation, bribery, corruption, or convincing that can change their reflection. Horses never lie. Can I bear the reflection? As a leader—as a mother, partner, and human—not only is it my responsibility to create those conditions but to be willing to face the truth when I am not.

And when, on a magnificent Sunday afternoon, I suddenly tap into their explosive joy while galloping along a ridgeline and changing leads midflight, can I stay astride the atomic blast beneath me? Or will I try to subvert it, tame it somehow, make it more manageable? Can I keep my seat at the center of their fire? If so, I participate in hands-down the most ecstatically liberating moment with another being. Joy is such a power.

Our leaders need to bear the same reflection and remain seated in the wonderfully wild ride of their life if they do. Are their countries joyful? Their organizations? They need to be prepared to hear the truth. Are we willing to tell it to them? Imagine a world where we appointed, hired, and elected our leaders by their ability to create conditions that would liberate the transformative power of joy. Imagine a world in which education was charged with forging joyful young people and parents were supported in creating joyful households, rather than slogging through homework all night, harnessed to the wheel of increasing work demands.

It's a *flying* lead change we need, not just change. We need elemental levity—a gravity-defying change of balance, outside of what we've been culturally instructed to think and do. Joy is a propulsive and levitative force, and anything that gathers and channels that energy threatens to upend the rigid control of a population. Joyful expressions such as music, dance, affection, laughter, art, theatre, eroticism—all of these fuel an exalted emotional response that creates momentum fueled by the divine, one that cannot be controlled. Take for example the Singing Revolution—a series of protests involving mass singing demonstrations that swept across Latvia, Lithuania, and Estonia between 1987 and 1991, eventually leading to their independence from the Soviet Union.[5]

As I come to the close of the ten-month journey of writing this book and of pulling together a lifetime of notes, essays, and research, I find myself pausing to find the final perfect story of how the horses have evoked and taught joy. Then it suddenly occurs to me that every single EQUUS session we have ever facilitated culminates in joy. The horses, without fail, ensure that joy is both the process and the outcome. In an ordinary sand arena, there under the vast electric-blue northern New Mexico sky, at the foothills of the Sangre de Cristo mountains, joy is born, each and every day.

This is now our challenge together—to lead our lives and lead others by creating the essential conditions of safety, connection, peace, and freedom through our care and presence, so that we can create a joyful world. Each one of us emerged from indigenous roots, informed by wisdom. We can reclaim our memory and membership to those lineages. Living according to the ancient way, a nature-informed way, is not a throwback; the ancient way is not old, but eternal. Nature is always acutely contemporary and leaning into the emergent future. When we are called, we are called to return to our natural state to the source of joy itself, to serve joy in a contemporary world.

It is my experience that the prophecy of "The Promise" is true, that the horses came to us to be our venerable companions toward making the right choice—a noble role handed to them for 56 million years by a 3.8 billion-year-old successful system, Mother Nature, born of the universe itself. Will we take on the mantle of wisdom now being passed down to us through these sacred hands?

Uncle Bob was right when he nodded toward the wild horses in Australia so many years ago and told me that they would take me home.

They have. And they continue the spiraled journey with me toward ever more meaningful realms. So now I say the same to you, with a nod toward the horses and all the ancient wisdom behind them and all the nature surrounding them, spiraling out into the universe as an eternal symbol of our co-evolutionary heart:

That mob out there . . . they'll get you home.

GIVING BACK

A portion of the proceeds of this book are donated to Tewa Women United, a multicultural and multiracial organization founded and led by Native women located in the ancestral Tewa homelands of northern New Mexico. TWU protects and lifts up the voices of indigenous women and works to heal the traumatic effects of colonization, religious inquisition, and militarization leading to issues such as alcoholism, suicide, domestic/sexual violence, and environmental violence. For more information please visit tewawomenunited.org.

GRATITUDE

A book is a community made manifest, and this one would have never happened without so many who have contributed to these pages. To the community of people around the world who care every day to make the world a better place, whether you are raising a compassionate child, volunteering at a nonprofit, or leading a conscious company, every single action you make, no matter how small, makes a difference. You inspire me, you make me proud to be human, you provoke me to be a better human. To you, the reader, for being an important member of that community. To the animals, trees, plants, rocks, rivers, mountains, deserts, and oceans, thank you for sustaining us and teaching us, though we are still finding our way. And especially, thank you to all the horses past, present, and future, such patient supreme mentors you are. I owe my entire life to you.

To all my teachers, human and otherwise, most importantly my equine spiritual masters Artemis, Blue, Brio, Dante, Cisco, and Kassie, and dear Cimarron (whom we lost tragically during the writing of this book). Thank you for mentoring me, loving me, and holding me to an integrity that is beyond earthly. Thank you for making me show up every day to do the work of translating your message. To my liberty mentors Louise Kropach and Frédéric Pignon. To the scientists who've inspired me: Rick Hanson, PhD, and James Prescott, PhD. To Tesuque Pueblo elder Kathy Sanchez for your counsel and for blessing our horses and our work.

Scott Strachan, my unicorn, your commitment to EQUUS and to our clients, and your belief in me, was the fuel behind every word in this book. Thank you for walking along this journey with me, for teaching me how to love, for taking on the extra work so I could write, for insisting I find my own voice, and for holding me close when things got dark, for showing me how to manifest dreams, and for encouraging me to never ever give up.

To three of the most amazing beings I know—my mother Peta, who was my first spiritual teacher (and I truly am the luckiest daughter); to my son Dakota, who taught me how to be a mother, who opens my mind and heart to new realms, and whose uncommon kindness and honesty inspires me every day; to my daughter MacKenzie who taught me how to listen, who opens my mind and heart to new worlds, and whose generous and spirited soul inspires me every day. You both make me a better human and continue to do so every day. To our dogs Molly and Katy, who run with me on rides and hikes, and wag at me all day.

I'm immensely grateful to my editor Buzzy Jackson, who believed in this book and in me, and who took the time to get to know the horses to learn from them first-hand what the book is about. Buzzy, you saw me and my work in ways that were essential to this book's maturation. I'm so thankful to Sounds True publishing, specifically Anastasia Pellouchoud, who first called me to see if I'd like to write a book, and to Jaime Schwalb for trusting my work and firmly guiding the book's evolution and betterment. Thank you to the whole Sounds True team (and their dogs), Jade Lascelles, Robert Lee, the art department, the marketing team, and all who are behind birthing a book into the world.

Thank you to my brother Scott Wendorf for helping me find the awesome title (Miller, sorry we couldn't go with *Why the Long Face?*) and for your thoughtful feedback on the manuscript. I also want to acknowledge my three amazing stepchildren—Lywyn Armitstead Shapiro, and Kiosh and Kalani Shapiro. You three taught me so much about love, and Kiosh, thank you for your brilliant eleventh-hour input. Dan Weil, your support, your terrific diagrams featured in *Flying Lead Change*, and your loyalty to EQUUS as a friend, creative wizard, and faculty member has been critical to EQUUS's success. Stephanie Handley, my wing woman and the best-assistant-on-Planet-Earth, thank you for fiercely protecting my time and for conquering the endnotes. God help anyone who gets between Stephanie and what she cares about! Laura Cockfield, thank you for the amazing headshots and for making photo-taking fun! And to Linda Kemper, who graciously gave me use of her casita in which to disappear from the world and go dark so I could finish the book.

I'm so grateful to the following dear friends, colleagues, and EQUUS faculty members, all flying-lead-change-agents in their own right, who read the manuscript with great care and discernment—Toby Herzlich (Tobes), for all the support, unconditional love, and the inspiration and profound discussions while climbing peaks and camping under stars; Ali Schultz, Elizabeth Mathews, Ramcharan, and Kendra Prescott, your gifted presence and constructive feedback were critical to the final development of *Flying Lead Change*, and I'm so glad you are part of the EQUUS team! To Micki McMillan and Pat Barlow, beloved friends and founders of Blue Mesa Group, who not only tapped me on the shoulder and insisted I become a certified master coach, but who shepherded me to its actualization. Thank you also for your important comments and edits in the manuscript.

This book would not have been possible without the entire EQUUS family listed here. For the courageous clients featured in these pages and those not, all of you weave the story of human virtue and humanity's capacity to be great. To our volunteers, Klassie Pino, Ash Gallegos, and Deb Miller, thank you for your care of our horses and of Scott and me. To EQUUS faculty, staff, and beloveds—Audrey Herrera, Rebecca Farr, Ken Tohee, and Thunder Bear Yates. Randy Weber, thank you for letting me experiment on you all these years (much of the EQUUS Experience is because of where we explored together) and for keeping our technology upright. To Niccole Toral and Tod DiCecco for your insight on spirit animals for this book and for lifting up the EQUUS work into the domain of the sacred, the ancestral, and the holy. I am deeply grateful to Mary Ann Menetry, dear friend, hiking and riding buddy, but also beloved to our horses. Your gift of healing and skilled mastery in ortho-bionomy has kept our herd (and our hearts) thriving. Keith Meriweather (you dark horse you), thank you for your masterful horse training, your mentoring, and for being one of the few true horsemen in the world. The horses thank you. To the good people at Keshi, especially Robin Dunlap and Bronwyn Foxbern, who bring the medicine of the animals to the public every day. To Lisa Reagan, who bravely took on the mantle of *Kindred* when I could no longer shepherd it. To Barbara Randall, Uncle Bob's beloved wife, who continues and protects his good work. And to Sandy Witbeck, who has done so very much: gave us dear Cimarron (Lefty), made it possible to train with Frédéric Pignon, and who literally helped save Thunderbird Ridge. Sandy, words are not enough.

I wish to honor and give thanks to the ancestors, elders, and custodians of the earth who came before us. To the storytellers who weave us all together. To Kabada, who opened the door to the *real world*. And finally, profound gratitude to Tjilpi Bob Randall. Thank you for pointing me the way home again when I was lost. Thank you for your trust and your time and your love. I hope you are happy with these pages. I love you Uncle Bob.

NOTES

A LETTER FROM THE AUTHOR

1. Rollin McCraty, *Science of the Heart, Volume 2: Exploring the Role of the Heart in Human Performance* (HeartMath Institute, 2015), 3–7.

2. Benjamin Gardner, Phillippa Lally, and Jane Wardle, "Making Health Habitual: The Psychology of 'Habit-Formation' and General Practice," *British Journal of General Practice* 62, no. 605 (December 2012): 664–666, doi.org/10.3399/bjgp12X659466.

EPIGRAPH

1. Bev Doolittle, Jay Doolittle, and Elise MacLay. This poem, quoted in full, is one aspect of a mixed-media collaboration between the three artists cited. Used with permission.

INTRODUCTION

1. Asafa Jalata, *Oromia and Ethiopia: State Formation and Ethnonational Conflict, 1868–1992* (Boulder, CO: Lynne Rienner Publishers, 1993).

2. Yvette Running Horse Collin, "The Relationship Between the Indigenous Peoples of the Americas and the Horse: Deconstructing a Eurocentric Myth" (PhD diss., University of Alaska Fairbanks, 2017).

3. Iain McGilchrist, in the RSA's "The Divided Brain," YouTube video, 11:47, October 21, 2011, youtube.com/watch?v=dFs9WO2B8uI.

4. Ken Ashwell, ed., *Neurobiology of Monotremes: Brain Evolution in Our Distant Mammalian Cousins* (Australia: CSIRO Publishing, 2013), 2.

5. Anna-Sapfo Malaspinas et al., "A Genomic History of Aboriginal Australia," *Nature* 538 (Oct 2016): 207–214, doi.org/10.1038/nature18299.

6. *Bringing Them Home: Report of the National Inquiry into the Separation of Aboriginal and Torres Strait Islander Children from Their Families* (Sydney: Human Rights and Equal Opportunity Commission, 1997).

7. A. O. Neville, "Coloured Folk: Some Pitiful Cases," *The West Australian* (April 18, 1930), 9.

PART I: LEARNING TO LISTEN

1. David Whyte, "The Winter of Listening," *The House of Belonging: Poems* (Langley, WA: Many Rivers Press, 1997), 29.

CHAPTER 1: THE PROMISE

1. Robin Wall Kimmerer, *Braiding Sweetgrass: Indigenous Wisdom, Scientific Knowledge, and the Teachings of Plants* (Minneapolis: Milkweed Editions, 2013), 7.

2. Yvette Running Horse Collin, "The Relationship Between the Indigenous Peoples of the Americas and the Horse: Deconstructing a Eurocentric Myth" (PhD diss., University of Alaska Fairbanks, 2017), 123.

3. Wendy Williams, *The Horse: The Epic History of Our Noble Companion* (New York: Farrar, Straus, and Giroux, 2015), 49–51.

4. Williams, *The Horse*, 49–51.

5. Williams, *The Horse*, 49–51.

6. Williams, *The Horse*, 49–51.

7. Cristina Luis et al., "Iberian Origins of New World Horse Breeds," *Journal of Heredity* 97, no. 2 (March/April 2006): 107–113, doi.org/10.1093/jhered/esj020.

8. Collin, "The Relationship Between the Indigenous Peoples of the Americas and the Horse," 133–167.

9. Kimmerer, *Braiding Sweetgrass*, 9.

10. Toby Herzlich, at Festival of Faiths 2019, "What Would Nature Do?" YouTube video, 27:48, May 14, 2019, youtube.com/watch?v=n3ClyFzQOkA.

11. Michael Pollan, *The Botany of Desire: A Plant's-Eye View of the World* (New York: Random House, 2002), xiv–xxi.

12. Pollan, *The Botany of Desire*.

PART II: CARE

1. Wendell Berry, *The Art of the Commonplace: The Agrarian Essays of Wendell Berry* (Berkeley: Counterpoint, 2002), 63.

CHAPTER 3: KANYINI

1. Kanyini Care Diagram inspired by Kim Scott's *Radical Candor: Be a Kick-Ass Boss Without Losing Your Humanity* (New York: St. Martin's Press, 2017), in which she encourages readers to "care personally" and "challenge directly" with her Radical Candor framework.

CHAPTER 4: CONSERVATION OF ENERGY

1. John Elder and Hertha D. Wong, eds., *Family of Earth and Sky: Indigenous Tales of Nature from Around the World* (Boston: Beacon Press, 1994), 50–51. Used with permission.

PART III: PRESENCE

1. Peter Senge et al., *Presence: An Exploration of Profound Change in People, Organizations, and Society* (New York: Doubleday, 2005), 50.

CHAPTER 5: BEINGNESS

1. Arthur Osborne, ed., *The Teachings of Ramana Maharshi* (York Beach, ME: Samuel Weiser, Inc., 1996), 9–10.

2. David Godman, ed., *Be As You Are: The Teachings of Sri Ramana Maharshi* (London: Penguin Books, 1985).

3. Godman, *Be As You Are.*

4. Godman, *Be As You Are.*

5. Dan Siegel, *Aware: The Science and Practice of Presence—The Groundbreaking Meditation Practice* (New York: Penguin, 2018), 3–4.

6. Siegel, *Aware.*

7. Godman, *Be As You Are.*

CHAPTER 6: EMERGENCE

1. Peter Senge et al., *Presence: An Exploration of Profound Change in People, Organizations, and Society* (New York: Doubleday, 2005), 50.

2. C. Otto Scharmer, *Theory U: Leading from the Future as It Emerges* (Oakland, CA: Berrett-Koehler, 2009), 18–20.

3. Senge et al., *Presence.*

4. Robert and Michele Root-Bernstein, "Einstein On Creative Thinking: Music and the Intuitive Art of Scientific Imagination," *Psychology Today*, March 31, 2010, psychologytoday.com/us/blog/imagine/201003 /einstein-creative-thinking-music-and-the-intuitive -art-scientific-imagination.

PART IV: SAFETY

1. Clarissa Pinkola Estés, *Women Who Run With the Wolves: Myths and Stories of the Wild Woman Archetype* (New York: Random House, 1996), 45. Note: I changed the genders here from "a woman" to "a person" and from "her" to "their."

CHAPTER 8: SPACE

1. Michael S. A. Graziano, *The Spaces Between Us: A Story of Neuroscience, Evolution, and Human Nature* (New York: Oxford University Press, 2018), ix.

2. Graziano, *The Spaces Between Us*, 1.

3. Graziano, *The Spaces Between Us*, 24.

4. Graziano, *The Spaces Between Us*, 22–23.

5. Graziano, *The Spaces Between Us*, 17.

6. Bessel van der Kolk, *The Body Keeps the Score: Brain, Mind, and Body in the Healing of Trauma* (New York: Penguin Books, 2015), 97.

7. Antonio R. Damasio, *The Feeling of What Happens: Body and Emotion in the Making of Consciousness* (New York: Harcourt Brace, 1999), 28.

8. 1 Corinthians 9:27 (English Standard Version).

9. Van der Kolk, *The Body Keeps the Score*.

10. Amy Cuddy, "Your Body Language May Shape Who You Are," filmed June 2012, TED video, 20:48, ted.com/talks/amy_cuddy_your_body_language_may _shape_who_you_are.

11. William Blake, "The Little Black Boy," *Poems and Prophecies* (New York: Dutton, 1970).

CHAPTER 9: PLACE

1. Gerald G. May, *The Awakened Heart: Opening Yourself to the Love You Need* (San Francisco: HarperCollins, 1993), 3–4.

2. Brené Brown, *Daring Greatly: How the Courage to Be Vulnerable Transforms the Way We Live, Love, Parent, and Lead* (New York: Avery, 2015), 67.

3. Brown, *Daring Greatly*.

4. Patrick Minges, "Beneath the Underdog: Race, Religion, and the Trail of Tears," *American Indian Quarterly* 25, no. 3 (2001): 454–79, jstor.org/stable/1185862?seq=1.

5. Mario Martinez, "The MindBody Code, Part 1," interview by Tami Simon, *Insights at the Edge,* November 18, 2014, resources.soundstrue.com/podcast /the-mindbody-code-part-1.

CHAPTER 10:
LEADING FROM BEHIND

1. Dick Leonard, *The Great Rivalry: Gladstone and Disraeli* (London: I. B. Tauris, 2013).

PART V: CONNECTION

1. Alan Watts, *The Book: On the Taboo Against Knowing Who You Are* (New York: Vintage Books, 1989), 9.

2. Cigna, "New Cigna Study Reveals Loneliness at Epidemic Levels in America," *Business Wire,* May 1, 2018, businesswire.com/news/home/20180501005804/en /New-Cigna-Study-Reveals-Loneliness-Epidemic-Levels.

3. Julianne Holt-Lunstad et al., "Loneliness and Social Isolation as Risk Factors for Mortality: A Meta-Analytic Review," *Perspectives on Psychological Science* 10, no. 2 (March 2015): 227–37, doi.org/10.1177/1745691614568352.

CHAPTER 11: BELONGING

1. Harry F. Harlow, Robert O. Dodsworth, and Margaret K. Harlow, "Total Social Isolation in Monkeys," *Proceedings of the National Academy of Sciences of the United States of America* 54, no. 1 (1965): 90–97.

2. Mary D. Ainsworth et al., "Deprivation of Maternal Care: A Reassessment of Its Effects," *Public Health Papers* 14 (1962): 97–165; Sarah Blaffer Hrdy, *Mother Nature:*

Maternal Instincts and How They Shape the Human Species
(New York: Ballantine Books, 2000).

3. James W. Prescott, "The Origins of Human Love and Violence," *Pre- and Perinatal Psychology Journal* 10, no. 3 (Spring 1996): 143–188.

4. Marcia Mikulak, *The Children of a Bambara Village* (paper, University of North Dakota, 1975), 18.

5. Robert Wolff, *Original Wisdom: Stories of an Ancient Way of Knowing* (Rochester, VT: Inner Traditions/Bear, 2001), 111–197.

6. Wolff, *Original Wisdom*, 193; 196–97.

7. Richard Louv, "Animals Are the Cure for Loneliness," *Outside*, September 1, 2018, outsideonline.com /2339706/animals-cure-loneliness.

8. Diana E. Bowler et al., "A Systematic Review of Evidence for the Added Benefits to Health of Exposure to Natural Environments," *BMC Public Health* 456 (2010), doi.org/10.1186/1471-2458-10-456; Alexandra Sifferlin, "The Healing Power of Nature," *Time* (July 14, 2016), time.com/4405827/the-healing-power-of -nature; Florence Williams, "Call to the Wild: This is Your Brain on Nature," *National Geographic* (July 25, 2017), nationalgeographic.com/magazine/2016/01 /call-to-wild.

9. US Department of Health and Human Services, "Unaccompanied Alien Children (UAC) Program," fact sheet (updated October 31, 2019), hhs.gov /sites/default/files/unaccompanied-alien-children -program-fact-sheet-01-2020.pdf.

CHAPTER 13: VULNERABILITY

1. Brené Brown, *Daring Greatly: How the Courage to Be Vulnerable Transforms the Way We Live, Love, Parent, and Lead* (New York: Avery, 2015), 34.

2. Elana Lyn Gross, "Inside the Insanely Competitive World of Elite New York City Preschools," *Business Insider* (June 14, 2018), businessinsider.com /preschools-in-new-york-city-2018-6.

3. Brené Brown, "The Power of Vulnerability," filmed June 2010, TEDxHouston video, 20:49, youtube.com /watch?v=iCvmsMzlF7o.

4. Terry Tempest Williams, "A Conversation with Terry Tempest Williams," interview by Penguin Random House on her book *Leap*, penguinrandomhouse.com/books /191447/leap-by-terry-tempest-williams/9780679752578.

CHAPTER 14:
ENGAGING THE INVISIBLES

1. Antoine de Saint Exupéry, *The Little Prince* (Orlando: Harcourt, 2000), 53.

2. Fritjof Capra, *The Tao of Physics: An Exploration of the Parallels between Modern Physics and Eastern Mysticism* (Boston: Shambhala Publications, 1999), 68.

3. Lisa Reagan, "Spiritual Composting: A Prodigal Daughter's Return," *Kindred* 23 (September 2007).

4. Eckhart Tolle, "How Do I Keep From Being Triggered?" YouTube video, 16:31, February 8, 2019, youtube.com /watch?v=lAaBXlC8-bU.

5. Robin Wall Kimmerer, *Braiding Sweetgrass: Indigenous Wisdom, Scientific Knowledge, and the Teachings of Plants* (Minneapolis: Milkweed Editions, 2013), 55.

6. Lynn Ungar, "Boundaries," *Blessing the Bread: Meditations* (Boston: Skinner House Books, 1996), 3–4.

PART VI: PEACE

1. Marianne Williamson (@mariwilliamson), "Ego says, 'Once everything falls into place, I'll feel peace.'

Spirit says, 'Find your peace, and then everything will fall into place.'" Twitter, August 10, 2013, twitter.com /marwilliamson/status/366263645572829185?lang=en.

2. David Forbes, *Mindfulness and Its Discontents: Education, Self, and Social Transformation* (Halifax: Fernwood Publishing, Limited, 2019), 25.

CHAPTER 15: CONGRUENCE

1. Catherine Lizette Gonzalez, "In 'Pleasure Activism,' Adrienne Maree Brown Dares Us to Get in Touch with Our Needs," *Colorlines*, February 26, 2019, colorlines .com/articles/pleasure-activism-adrienne-maree-brown -dares-us-get-touch-our-needs.

2. Pema Chödrön, *Awakening Loving-Kindness* (Boston: Shambhala Publications, 1996), 82.

3. Chödrön, *Awakening Loving-Kindness*, 83.

CHAPTER 16: TEMPO

1. Ecclesiastes 3:1 (American Standard Version).

2. Larry Littlebird bio, Hamaatsa website, hamaatsa.org /LarryLittlebird.html.

3. *The Biggest Little Farm*, a documentary film directed by John Chester (NEON, May 10, 2019), 1:31.

PART VII: FREEDOM

1. H. W. L. Poonja, *The Truth Is* (Newburyport, MA: Red Wheel/Weiser, 2000), 20.

CHAPTER 17: REWILDING

1. Clarissa Pinkola Estés, *Women Who Run With the Wolves: Myths and Stories of the Wild Woman Archetype* (New York: Random House, 1996), 278–282.

2. Mario Martinez, "The MindBody Code, Part 1," interview by Tami Simon, *Insights at the Edge*,

November 18, 2014, resources.soundstrue.com /podcast/the-mindbody-code-part-1/.

3. Martinez, "The MindBody Code, Part 1."

4. Niccole Toral, email conversation with author, August 14, 2019.

5. Robin Dunlap, email conversation with author, May 20, 2017.

6. Mary Oliver, "Wild Geese," *Dream Work* (New York: The Atlantic Monthly Press, 1986).

CHAPTER 18: CREATION

1. Marion Miller, personal conversation with author, October 6, 2018.

2. John 1:1 (English Standard Version).

3. Christian Jarrett, "The Transformational Power of How You Talk About Your Life," *BBC Future* (May 26, 2019), bbc.com/future/article/20190523-the-way-you-tell -your-life-story-shapes-your-personality.

4. Julia Butterfly Hill, "The Taoist and the Activist," interview by Benjamin Tong, *Lunch with Bokara*, KCET video, 28:23, kcet.org/shows/lunch-with-bokara /episodes/the-taoist-and-the-activist.

5. Howard Zinn, "The Optimism of Uncertainty," *The Nation* (September 2, 2004), thenation.com/article/ optimism-uncertainty.

6. David Sheff, *All We Are Saying: The Last Major Interview with John Lennon and Yoko Ono* (New York: St. Martin's Press, 2000), 212–13.

CHAPTER 19: LIBERATION

1. Chögyam Trungpa, *The Lion's Roar: An Introduction to Tantra* (Boston: Shambhala Publications, 2001), 20.

2. Trungpa, *The Lion's Roar*, 28.

3. Trungpa, *The Lion's Roar*, 28.

4. David Whyte, "Heartbreak," *Consolations: The Solace, Nourishment, and Underlying Meaning of Everyday Words* (Langley, WA: Many Rivers Press, 2015), 104–105.

PART VIII: JOY

1. Pema Chödrön, *When Things Fall Apart: Heart Advice for Difficult Times* (Boston: Shambhala Publications, 2005), 119.

CHAPTER 20:
THE BODY AS A VEHICLE FOR JOY

1. James W. Prescott, "The Prescott Report," *NIH Violence Research: Historical Perspectives and Future Directions* (June 21, 1993), violence.de/Prescott/report/part1.html.

2. James W. Prescott, "How Culture Shapes the Developing Brain and the Future of Humanity," *Kindred* 9 (March 2004).

3. James W. Prescott, "Body Pleasures and the Origins of Violence," *Bulletin of the Atomic Scientists* (November 1975): 10–20.

4. Charles Darwin, *The Expression of the Emotions in Man and Animals* (Belgium: Greenwood Press, 1969), 76.

5. Catherine Lizette Gonzalez, "In 'Pleasure Activism,' Adrienne Maree Brown Dares Us to Get in Touch with Our Needs," *Colorlines*, February 26, 2019, colorlines .com/articles/pleasure-activism-adrienne-maree -brown-dares-us-get-touch-our-needs.

6. John Krakauer, "Why Do We Like to Dance—And Move to the Beat?" *Scientific American* (September 26, 2008), scientificamerican.com/article/experts-dance.

7. Scott Edwards, "Dancing and the Brain," *On the Brain* (Harvard Mahoney Neuroscience Institute newsletter), Sept. 2017, neuro.hms.harvard.edu/harvard-mahoney

-neuroscience-institute/brain-newsletter/and-brain
-series/dancing-and-brain.

8. Stacy Horn, "Singing Changes Your Brain," *Time*,
August 16, 2013, ideas.time.com/2013/08/16
/singing-changes-your-brain.

9. Audre Lorde, *A Burst of Light and Other Essays* (Ithaca,
NY: Firebrand Books, 1988), 130.

CHAPTER 21:
LEADING THE FLYING CHANGE

1. John Womack, Jr., ed., *Rebellion in Chiapas: An Historical
Reader* (New York: New Press, 1999), 303.

2. Brittany Packnett, "I'm an Activist, and Joy is My
Resistance," *Self*, August 21, 2017, self.com/story
/Charlottesville-joy-is-resistance.

3. Ursula K. Le Guin, "The Ones Who Walk Away from
Omelas," *The Wind's Twelve Quarters: Stories* (New York:
William Morrow, 2004), 278.

4. Tewa Women United, tewawomenunited.org/about/.

5. Allison Brooks-Conrad, "Sounds of the Singing
Revolution: Alo Mattiisen, Popular Music, and the
Estonian Independence Movement, 1987–1991,"
(Honors project, Lawrence University, 2018),
lux.lawrence.edu/luhp/124.

ABOUT THE AUTHOR

Kelly Wendorf is a mother and International Coach Federation Master Certified Coach (MCC) who specializes in transformative change, author, spiritual mentor, horsewoman, and socially responsible entrepreneur. She is the founding partner of EQUUS, an innovative leadership development organization that she runs with her partner J. Scott Strachan. EQUUS uniquely combines neuroscience, systems theory, contemplative wisdom, attachment theory, somatic processes, indigenous knowledge, and nature-based intelligence in its coaching and experiential leadership development approach. Kelly's work has been featured in such publications as *Forbes, WSJ: The Wall Street Journal Magazine, Vogue*, and *Huffington Post*, and has been the inspiration for several award-winning documentaries. She lives in Santa Fe, New Mexico with Scott, Molly, and Katy the dogs, two barn cats, and seven equines. For more on Kelly and her work, please visit equusinspired.com and kellywendorf.com.

ABOUT SOUNDS TRUE

Sounds True is a multimedia publisher whose mission is to inspire and support personal transformation and spiritual awakening. Founded in 1985 and located in Boulder, Colorado, we work with many of the leading spiritual teachers, thinkers, healers, and visionary artists of our time. We strive with every title to preserve the essential "living wisdom" of the author or artist. It is our goal to create products that not only provide information to a reader or listener, but that also embody the quality of a wisdom transmission.

For those seeking genuine transformation, Sounds True is your trusted partner. At SoundsTrue.com you will find a wealth of free resources to support your journey, including exclusive weekly audio interviews, free downloads, interactive learning tools, and other special savings on all our titles.

To learn more, please visit SoundsTrue.com/freegifts or call us toll-free at 800.333.9185.